Declaration

Michael Hardt and Antonio Negri

ISBN: 9780786752904
eISBN : 9780786752911

Cover design by Benjamin Shaykin

Distributed by Argo Navis Author Services

Opening: Take Up the Baton

This is not a manifesto. Manifestos provide a glimpse of a world to come and also call into being the subject, who although now only a specter must materialize to become the agent of change. Manifestos work like the ancient prophets, who by the power of their vision create their own people. Today's social movements have reversed the order, making manifestos and prophets obsolete. Agents of change have already descended into the streets and occupied city squares, not only threatening and toppling rulers but also conjuring visions of a new world. More important, perhaps, the multitudes, through their logics and practices, their slogans and desires, have declared a new set of principles and truths. How can their declaration become the basis for constituting a new and sustainable society? How can those principles and truths guide us in reinventing how we relate to each other and our world? In their rebellion, the multitudes must discover the passage from declaration to constitution.

Early in 2011, in the depths of social and economic crises characterized by radical inequality, common sense seemed to dictate that we trust the decisions and guidance of the ruling powers, lest even greater disasters befall us. The financial and governmental rulers may be tyrants, and they may have been primarily responsible for creating the crises, but we had no choice. During the course of 2011, however, a series of social struggles shattered that common sense and began to construct a new one. Occupy Wall Street was the most visible but was only one moment in a cycle of struggles that shifted the terrain of political debate and opened new possibilities for political action over the course of the year.

Two thousand eleven began early. On 17 December 2010 in Sidi Bouzid, Tunisia, twenty-six-year-old street vendor Mohamed Bouazizi, who was reported to have earned a computer science degree, set himself on fire. By the end of the month, mass revolts had spread to Tunis with the demand, "Ben Ali dégage!" and indeed by the middle of January, Zine el-Abidine Ben Ali was already gone. Egyptians took up the baton and, with tens and hundreds of thousands regularly coming out in the streets starting in late January, demanded that Hosni Mubarak go too. Cairo's Tahrir Square was occupied for a mere eighteen days before Mubarak departed.

Protests against repressive regimes spread quickly to other countries in North Africa and the Middle East, including Bahrain and Yemen and eventually Libya and Syria, but the initial spark in Tunisia and Egypt also caught fire farther away. The protesters occupying the Wisconsin statehouse in February and March expressed solidarity and recognized resonance with their counterparts in Cairo, but the crucial step began on 15 May in the occupations of central squares in Madrid and Barcelona by the so-called *indignados*. The Spanish encampments took inspiration from the Tunisian and Egyptian revolts and carried forward their struggles in new ways. Against the socialist-led government of José Luis Rodríguez Zapatero, they demanded, "Democracia real ya," refusing the representation of all political parties, and they forwarded a wide range of social protests, from the corruption of the banks to unemployment, from the lack of social services to insufficient housing and the injustice of evictions. Millions of Spaniards participated in the movement, and the vast majority of the population supported their demands. In occupied squares the *indignados* formed assemblies for decision-making and investigative commissions to explore a range of social issues.

Even before the encampments in Madrid's Puerta del Sol were dismantled in June, the Greeks had taken up the baton from the *indignados* and occupied Syntagma Square in Athens to protest against austerity measures. Not long after, tents sprang up on Tel Aviv's Rothschild Boulevard to demand social justice and welfare for Israelis. In early August, after police shot a black Briton, riots broke out in Tottenham and spread throughout England.

When a few hundred pioneer occupiers brought their tents to New York's Zuccotti Park on 17 September, then, it was their turn to take up the baton. And indeed their actions and the spread of the movements in the United States and across the world have to be understood with the year's experiences at their backs.

Many who are not part of the struggles have trouble seeing the connections in this list of events. The North African rebellions opposed repressive regimes and their demands centered on the removal of tyrants, whereas the wide-ranging social demands of the encampments in Europe, the United States, and Israel addressed representative constitutional systems. Furthermore, the Israeli tent protest (don't call it an occupation!) delicately balanced demands so as to remain silent about questions of settlements and Palestinian rights; the Greeks are facing sovereign debt and austerity measures of historic proportions; and the indignation of the British rioters addressed a long history of racial hierarchy—and they didn't even pitch tents.

Each of these struggles is singular and oriented toward specific local conditions. The first thing to notice, though, is that they did, in fact, speak to one another. The Egyptians, of course, clearly moved down paths traveled by the Tunisians and adopted their slogans, but the occupiers of Puerta del Sol also thought of their struggle as carrying on the experiences of those at Tahrir. In turn, the eyes of those in Athens and Tel Aviv were focused on the experiences of Madrid and Cairo. The Wall Street occupiers had them all in view, translating, for instance, the struggle against the tyrant into a struggle against the tyranny of finance. You may think that they were just deluded and forgot or ignored the differences in their situations and demands. We believe, however, that they have a clearer vision than those outside the struggle, and they can hold together without contradiction their singular conditions and local battles with the common global struggle.

Ralph Ellison's invisible man, after an arduous journey through a racist society, developed the ability to communicate with others in struggle. "Who knows," Ellison's narrator concludes, "but that, on the lower frequencies, I speak for you?" Today, too, those in struggle communicate on the lower frequencies, but, unlike in Ellison's time, no one speaks for them. The lower frequencies are open airwaves for all. And some messages can be heard only by those in struggle.

These movements do, of course, share a series of characteristics, the most obvious of which is the strategy of encampment or occupation. A decade ago the alterglobalization movements were nomadic. They migrated from one summit meeting to the next, illuminating the injustices and antidemocratic nature of a series of key institutions of the global power system: the World Trade Organization, the International Monetary Fund, the World Bank, and the G8 national leaders, among others. The cycle of struggles that began in 2011, in contrast, is sedentary. Instead of roaming according to the calendar of the summit meetings, these movements stay put and, in fact, refuse to move. Their immobility is partly due to the fact that they are so deeply rooted in local and national social issues.

The movements also share their internal organization as a multitude. The foreign press corps searched desperately in Tunisia and Egypt for a leader of the movements. During the most intense period of the Tahrir Square occupation, for example, they would each day presume a different figure was the *real* leader: one day it was Mohamed ElBaradei, the Nobel Prize winner, the next day Google executive Wael Ghonim, and so forth. What the media couldn't understand or accept was that there was no leader in Tahrir Square. The movements' refusal to have a leader was recognizable throughout the year but perhaps was most pronounced in Wall Street. A series of intellectuals and celebrities made appearances at Zuccotti Park, but no one could consider any of them leaders; they were guests of the multitude. From Cairo and Madrid to Athens and New York, the movements instead developed horizontal mechanisms for organization. They didn't build headquarters or form central committees but spread out like swarms, and most important, they created democratic practices of decision making so that all participants could lead together.

A third characteristic that the movements exhibit, albeit in different ways, is what we conceive as a struggle for the common. In some cases this has been expressed in flames. When Mohamed Bouazizi set himself on fire, his protest was understood to be against not only the abuse he suffered at the hands of the local police but also the widely shared social and economic plight of workers in the country, many of whom are unable to find work adequate to their education. Indeed in both Tunisia and Egypt the loud calls to remove the tyrant made many observers deaf to the profound social and economic issues at stake in the movements, as well as the crucial actions of the trade unions. The August fires of rioting in London also expressed protest against the current economic and social order. Like the Parisian rioters in 2005 and those in Los Angeles more than a decade before, the indignation of Britons responded to a complex set of social issues, the most central of which is racial subordination. But the burning and looting in each of these cases also responds to the power of commodities and the rule of property, which are themselves, of course, often vehicles of racial subordination. These are struggles for the common, then, in the sense that they contest the injustices of neoliberalism and, ultimately, the rule of private property. But that does not make them socialist. In fact, we see very little of traditional socialist movements in this cycle of struggles. And as much as struggles for the common contest the rule of private property, they equally oppose the rule of public property and the control of the state.

In this pamphlet we aim to address the desires and accomplishments of the cycle of struggles that erupted in 2011, but we do so not by analyzing them directly. Instead we begin by investigating the general social and political conditions in which they arise. Our point of attack here is the dominant forms of subjectivity produced in the context of the current social and political crisis. We engage four primary subjective figures—the indebted, the mediatized, the securitized, and the represented—all of which are impoverished and their powers for social action are masked or mystified.

Movements of revolt and rebellion, we find, provide us the means not only to refuse the repressive regimes under which these subjective figures suffer but also to invert these subjectivities in figures of power. They discover, in other words, new forms of independence and security on economic as well as social and communicational terrains, which together create the potential to throw off systems of political representation and assert their own powers of democratic action. These are some of the accomplishments that the movements have already realized and can develop further.

To consolidate and heighten the powers of such subjectivities, though, another step is needed. The movements, in effect, already provide a series of constitutional principles that can be the basis for a constituent process. One of the most radical and far-reaching elements of this cycle of movements, for example, has been the rejection of representation and the construction instead of schemas of democratic participation. These movements also give new meanings to freedom, our relation to the common, and a series of central political arrangements, which far exceed the bounds of the current republican constitutions. These meanings are now already becoming part of a new common sense. They are foundational principles that we already take to be inalienable rights, like those that were heralded in the course of the eighteenth-century revolutions.

The task is not to codify new social relations in a fixed order, but instead to create a constituent process that organizes those relations and makes them lasting while also fostering future innovations and remaining open to the desires of the multitude. The movements have declared a new independence, and a constituent power must carry that forward.

Chapter 1: Subjective Figures of the Crisis

The triumph of neoliberalism and its crisis have shifted the terms of economic and political life, but they have also operated a social, anthropological transformation, fabricating new figures of subjectivity. The hegemony of finance and the banks has produced *the indebted*. Control over information and communication networks has created *the mediatized*. The security regime and the generalized state of exception have constructed a figure prey to fear and yearning for protection—*the securitized*. And the corruption of democracy has forged a strange, depoliticized figure, *the represented*. These subjective figures constitute the social terrain on which—and against which—movements of resistance and rebellion must act. We will see later that these movements have the ability not only to refuse these subjectivities but also to invert them and create figures that are capable of expressing their independence and their powers of political action. First, though, we need to investigate the nature of the subjective figures of the neoliberal crisis.

The Indebted

Being in debt is becoming today the general condition of social life. It is nearly impossible to live without incurring debts—a student loan for school, a mortgage for the house, a loan for the car, another for doctor bills, and so on. The social safety net has passed from a system of *welfare* to one of *debtfare*, as loans become the primary means to meet social needs. Your subjectivity is configured on the foundation of debt. You survive by making debts, and you live under the weight of your responsibility for them.

Debt controls you. It disciplines your consumption, imposing austerity on you and often reducing you to strategies of survival, but beyond that it even dictates your work rhythms and choices. If you finish university in debt, you must accept the first paid position offered in order to honor your debt. If you bought an apartment with a mortgage, you must be sure not to lose your job or take a vacation or a study leave from work. The effect of debt, like that of the work ethic, is to keep your nose to the grindstone. Whereas the work ethic is born within the subject, debt begins as an external constraint but soon worms its way inside. Debt wields a moral power whose primary weapons are responsibility and guilt, which can quickly become objects of obsession. You are responsible for your debts and guilty for the difficulties they create in your life. The indebted is an unhappy consciousness that makes guilt a form of life. Little by little, the pleasures of activity and creation are transformed into a nightmare for those who do not possess the means to enjoy their lives. Life has been sold to the enemy.

G. W. F. Hegel's master-slave dialectic reappears here but in a nondialectical form, because debt is not a negative that can enrich you if you rebel, nor a subordination that fosters a line of activity, nor an impulse of liberation, nor an attempt to pass over to a free activity. Debt can only deepen the impoverishment of your life and the depotentialization of your subjectivity. It only debases you, isolating you in guilt and misery. Debt thus puts an end to all the illusions that surround the dialectic—the illusion, for example, that the subjugated labor of the unhappy consciousness could achieve freedom or affirm its own power, wresting away the forces that had been denied it or, rather, that the expression of labor could be resolved in a superior synthesis and that the determinate negation could rise up to liberation. The figure of the indebted cannot be redeemed but only destroyed.

Once upon a time there was a mass of wage workers; today there is a multitude of precarious workers. The former were exploited by capital, but that exploitation was masked by the myth of a free and equal exchange among owners of commodities. The latter continue to be exploited, but the dominant image of their relationship to capital is configured no longer as an equal relationship of exchange but rather as a hierarchical relation of debtor to creditor. According to the mercantile myth of capitalist production, the owner of capital meets the owner of labor power in the marketplace, and they make a fair and free exchange: I give you my work and you give me a wage. This was the Eden, Karl Marx writes ironically, of "freedom, equality, property, and Bentham." There's no need for us to remind you how false and mystifying this supposed freedom and equality actually are.

But capitalist work relations have shifted. The center of gravity of capitalist production no longer resides in the factory but has drifted outside its walls. Society has become a factory, or rather, capitalist production has spread such that the labor power of the entire society tends to be subordinated to capitalist control. Capital increasingly exploits the entire range of our productive capacities, our bodies and our minds, our capacities for communication, our intelligence and creativity, our affective relations with each other, and more. Life itself has been put to work.

With this shift the primary engagement between capitalist and worker also changes. No longer is the typical scene of exploitation the capitalist overseeing the factory, directing and disciplining the worker in order to generate a profit. Today the capitalist is farther removed from the scene, and workers generate wealth more autonomously. The capitalist accumulates wealth primarily through rent, not profit—this rent most often takes a financial form and is guaranteed through financial instruments. This is where debt enters the picture, as a weapon to maintain and control the relationship of production and exploitation. Exploitation today is based primarily not on (equal or unequal) exchange but on debt, that is, on the fact that the 99 percent of the population is subject—owes work, owes money, owes obedience—to the 1 percent.

Debt obscures the productivity of workers but clarifies their subordination. Exploited work is cast in a mystified relationship—the wage regime—but its productivity is clearly measured according to the rule: labor time. Now, instead, productivity is ever more hidden as the divisions between work time and the time of life become increasingly blurred. In order to survive the indebted must sell his or her entire time of life. Those subject to debt in this way thus appear, even to themselves, primarily as consumers not producers. Yes, of course they produce, but they work to pay their debts, for which they are responsible because they consume. In contrast to the myth of equal exchange, then, the debtor-creditor relationship has the virtue of unmasking the vast inequalities at the foundation of capitalist society.

Once again, the movement we are tracing from exploitation to indebtedness corresponds to the transformation of capitalist production from an order based on the hegemony of profit (that is, the accumulation of the average value of industrial exploitation) to one dominated by rent (that is, by the average value of the exploitation of social development) and thus by the accumulation of the value socially produced in an increasingly abstract form. Production thus relies, in this passage, increasingly on socialized, not individual, figures of work, that is, on workers who immediately cooperate together prior to the discipline and control of the capitalist. The rentier is distant from the moment of the production of wealth and thus cannot perceive the cruel reality of exploitation, the violence of productive labor, and the suffering it causes in the production of rent. From Wall Street one doesn't see the suffering of each worker in the production of value, since that value tends to be based on the exploitation of a vast multitude, waged and unwaged. That all fades to gray in the financial control of life.

A new figure of the poor is emerging, which includes not only the unemployed and the precarious workers with irregular, part-time work, but also the stable waged workers and the impoverished strata of the so-called middle class. Their poverty is characterized primarily by the chains of debt. The increasing generality of indebtedness today marks a return to relations of servitude reminiscent of another time. And yet, much has changed.

Marx sardonically characterized the improved condition of proletarians who arose with the industrial age as *Vogelfrei*, free as birds insofar as they are doubly free of property. Proletarians are not the property of masters and thus are free of the medieval bonds of servitude (that is the good part), but also they are free of property in the sense that they have none. Today's new poor are still free in the second sense, but through their debt they are, once again, the property of masters, now masters who rule through finance. Reborn are the figures of the bondsman and the indentured servant. In an earlier era, immigrants and indigenous populations in the Americas and Australia had to work to buy themselves out of debt, but often their debt continually rose, condemning them to indefinite servitude. Unable to rise from the misery to which they are reduced, the indebted is bound by invisible chains that must be recognized, grasped, and broken order to become free.

The Mediatized

In previous eras it often appeared that in relation to the media political action was stifled primarily by the fact that people didn't have sufficient access to information or the means to communicate and express their own views. Indeed today repressive governments attempt to limit access to websites, close down blogs and Facebook pages, attack journalists, and generally block access to information. Countering such repression is certainly an important battle, and we have repeatedly witnessed how media networks and access to them eventually and inevitably overflow all such barriers, thwarting attempts to close and silence.

We are more concerned, though, about the ways that today's mediatized subjects suffer from the opposite problem, stifled by a surplus of information, communication, and expression. "The problem is no longer getting people to express themselves," Gilles Deleuze explains, "but providing little gaps of solitude and silence in which they might eventually find something to say. Repressive forces don't stop people from expressing themselves, but rather, force them to express themselves. What a relief to have nothing to say, the right to say nothing, because only then is there a chance of framing the rare, and ever rarer, the thing that might be worth saying." The problem of surplus, however, is not really homologous to the problem of lack, and it is not even a matter of quantity. Deleuze seems to be recalling here the political paradox highlighted by Étienne de La Boétie and Baruch Spinoza: sometimes people strive for their servitude as if it were their salvation. Is it possible that in their voluntary communication and expression, in their blogging and web browsing and social media practices, people are contributing to instead of contesting repressive forces? Instead of information and communication, Deleuze says, what we often need is the silence necessary for there to be thought. This is not really such a paradox. The aim is not really silence for Deleuze but having something worth saying. Primarily at stake in the question of political action and liberation, in other words, is not the quantity of information, communication, and expression but, rather, their quality.

The importance of information and communication in repressive apparatuses (or projects of liberation) is heightened by the fact that laboring practices and economic production are becoming ever more mediatized. Media and communications technologies are increasingly central to all types of productive practices and are key to the kinds of cooperation necessary for today's biopolitical production. For many workers, moreover, especially in the dominant countries, communications and social media seem simultaneously to free them from and chain them to their jobs. With your smart phone and your wireless connections, you can go anywhere and still be on the job, which you realize quickly means that anywhere you go you are still working! Mediatization is a major factor in the increasingly blurred divisions between work and life.

It thus seems more appropriate to think of such workers as not so much alienated as mediatized. Whereas the consciousness of the alienated worker is separated or divided, the consciousness of the mediatized is subsumed or absorbed in the web. The consciousness of the mediatized is not really split but fragmented and dispersed. The media, furthermore, don't really make you passive. In fact, they constantly call on you to participate, to choose what you like, to contribute your opinions, to narrate your life. The media are constantly responsive to your likes and dislikes, and in return you are constantly attentive. The mediatized is thus a subjectivity that is paradoxically neither active nor passive but rather constantly absorbed in attention.

How can we separate the repressive powers of media from the potential for liberation? Is it possible to recognize qualitative distinctions among different types of information and communication? Perhaps a look back at the role of information and communication in the factory in an earlier phase of production can give us some hints. In the early 1960s, Romano Alquati studied the kinds of information produced by workers in the Olivetti factory in Ivrea, Italy, and he found that workers produced a "valorizing information," whereas the bureaucracy of management produced an information of control. Matteo Pasquinelli translates Alquati's recognition into a distinction between living and dead information parallel to Marx's notion of living and dead labor: "*Living information* is continually produced by workers in order to be transformed into *dead information* and crystallized in the machines and the entire bureaucratic apparatus." There are thus at least two circuits of communication in the factory. Whereas the dead language of management and the machines codifies and reinforces the functioning of discipline and the relationships of subordination, the exchange of living information among workers can be mobilized in collective action and insubordination. Just as human productivity is masked in the figure of the indebted, in the figure of the mediatized resides mystified and depotentialized human intelligence. Or, better, the mediatized is full of dead information, suffocating our powers to create living information.

Marx makes a similar distinction among types of information and communication in an even earlier phase when he claims that the French peasantry in the mid-nineteenth century is not able to act as a class. He argues that since the peasants are dispersed across the countryside and cannot effectively communicate with one another, they are not capable of collective political action and, as he famously says, cannot represent themselves. The standard against which Marx measures rural peasant life here is that of the urban proletariat, which communicates and thus can act politically and represent itself as a class. It would be a mistake, however, to think of the information and communication that the peasants lack in Marx's view simply in terms of quantity. He is not saying that the peasants would not support Louis Bonaparte and disavow imperial dreams if they read all the newspapers and knew of his political intrigues, his wasteful wars, and his gambling debts. The most important communication the proletarians have, and that the peasants lack, is enacted in the physical, corporeal being together in the factory. The class and the bases of political action are formed not primarily through the circulation of information or even ideas but rather through the construction of political affects, which requires a physical proximity.

The encampments and occupations of 2011 have rediscovered this truth of communication. Facebook, Twitter, the Internet, and other kinds of communications mechanisms are useful, but nothing can replace the being together of bodies and the corporeal communication that is the basis of collective political intelligence and action. In all the occupations throughout the United States and around the world, from Rio de Janeiro to Ljubljana, from Oakland to Amsterdam, even in cases when they lasted only a short time, the participants experienced the power of creating new political affects through being together. Perhaps it is significant in this regard that the call to occupy Wall Street that appeared in *Adbusters* in the summer of 2011 was cast in artistic terms and was indeed heeded by, among others, artist collectives in New York. An occupation is a kind of happening, a performance piece that generates political affects.

The middle classes and the traditional Left also recognize how much we are integrated in media systems and how much we are impoverished by them, but the only response they can manage is a combination of nostalgia and old-fashioned Left moralism. They know that as media move ever deeper into our lives, from print and broadcast to electronic media, they create experiences that are increasingly superficial. The slow act of composing a personal letter to mail in the post has been almost entirely eclipsed by the rapidity and brevity of e-mail messages. Complex narratives of your life situation, longings, and desires have been reduced to the typical questions of social media: Where are you right now? What are you doing? The habits and practices of friendship have been diluted in the online procedure of "friending." Perhaps the extraordinarily widespread support for the occupations can be explained in part by the fact that the middle classes and the traditional Left recognize that the movements are attacking problems from which they also suffer but are incapable of addressing.

The Securitized

It's dizzying to think about all the information constantly being produced about you. You know, of course, that in certain places and situations surveillance is heightened. Pass through airport security, and your body and possessions will be scanned. Enter certain countries, and you will have your fingerprints taken, your retina scanned. Become unemployed, join the workfare regime, and there will be a different series of inspections, recording your efforts, your intentions, and your progress. The hospital, the government office, the school—they all have their own inspection regimes and data storage systems. But it's not only when you go somewhere special. A walk down your street is likely to be recorded by a series of security cameras, your credit card purchases and Internet searches are likely to be tracked, and your cell phone calls are easily intercepted. Security technologies have leapt forward in recent years to delve deeper into society, our lives, and our bodies.

Why do you accept being treated like an inmate? In a previous era the prison, separated from society, was the institution of total surveillance, whose inmates were constantly observed and their activities recorded, but today total surveillance is increasingly the general condition of society as a whole. "The prison," Michel Foucault notes, "begins well before its doors. It begins as soon as you leave your house"—and even before. Do you accept this because you are unaware of being watched? Or because you think you have no choice? Each of these may be true in part, but overlying both is fear. You accept being in a prison society because outside seems more dangerous.

You are not only the object of security but also the subject. You answer the call to be vigilant, constantly on watch for suspicious activity on the subway, devious designs of your seatmate on the airplane, malicious motives of your neighbors. Fear justifies volunteering your pair of eyes and your alert attention to a seemingly universal security machine.

There are two dramatis personae in securitized society: inmates and guards. And you are called to play both roles at once.

The securitized is a creature that lives and thrives in the state of exception, where the normal functioning of the rule of law and the conventional habits and bonds of association have been suspended by an overarching power. The state of exception is a state of war—today in some parts of the world this is a low-intensity war and in others it is rather high intensity, but everywhere the state of war promises no end. Don't confuse this state of exception with any natural condition of human society, and do not imagine it as the essence of the modern state or the end point toward which all modern figures of power are tending. No, the state of exception is a form of tyranny, one that, like all tyrannies, exists only because of our voluntary servitude.

To say that we are objects and subjects of surveillance like inmates and guards in a prison society does not mean that we are all in the same situation or that there is no longer a difference between being in prison and out. In recent decades, in fact, the number of those imprisoned across the world has expanded enormously, especially when one includes those not only in conventional prisons but also under judicial supervision, in detention centers, in refugee camps, and in myriad other forms of imprisonment.

It is a scandal—or, rather, it *should* be a scandal and one wonders why it isn't—that the US prison population, after reaching a postwar low in the early 1970s, has since grown more than 500 percent. The United States locks up a higher percentage of its own population than any other nation in the world. Even with extraordinary prison construction projects over the last decades, the cells are still overfull. This massive expansion cannot be explained by a growing criminality of the US population or the enhanced efficiency of law enforcement. In fact, US crime rates in this period have remained relatively constant.

The scandal of US prison expansion is even more dramatic when one observes how it operates along race divisions. Latinos are incarcerated at a rate almost double that of whites, and African Americans at a rate almost six times as high. The racial imbalance of those on death row is even more extreme. It is not hard to find shocking statistics. One in eight black US males in their twenties, for instance, is in jail or prison on any given day. The number of African Americans under correctional control today, Michelle Alexander points out, is greater than the number of slaves in the mid-nineteenth century. Some authors refer to the racially skewed prison expansion as a return to elements of the plantation system or the institution of new Jim Crow laws. Keep in mind that this differential racial pattern of imprisonment is not isolated to the United States. In Europe and elsewhere, if one considers immigrant detention centers and refugee camps as arms of the carceral apparatus, those with darker skin are disproportionately in captivity.

The securitized is thus not a homogeneous figure. In fact, the infinite degrees of incarceration are key to the functioning of securitized subjectivity. There are always others lower than you, under greater surveillance and control, even if only by the smallest degree.

During the same years of the prison expansion, there has also been a militarization of US society. What is most remarkable is not the growth in the number of soldiers in the United States but rather their social stature. Not too long ago, in the last years of the Vietnam War, it was rumored that protesters spit on returning soldiers and called them baby killers. This was probably a myth propagated to discredit the protesters, but it is indicative of the fact that soldiers and their social function were held then in low esteem. It is remarkable that only a few decades later military personnel have become (once again) objects of national reverence. Military personnel in uniform are given priority boarding on commercial airlines, and it is not uncommon for strangers to stop and thank them for their service. In the United States, rising esteem for the military in uniform corresponds to the growing militarization of the society as a whole. All of this despite repeated revelations of the illegality and immorality of the military's own incarceration systems, from Guantánamo to Abu Ghraib, whose systematic practices border on if not actually constitute torture.

The growth in prison populations and the rising militarization, both of which are led by US society, are only the most concrete, condensed manifestations of a diffuse security regime in which we are all interned and enlisted. Why are these trends taking place now? One phenomenon that corresponds historically with the rise of the security regime in its various forms is the predominance of neoliberal strategies of the capitalist economy. The increasing precarity, flexibility, and mobility of workers required by the neoliberal economy marks a new phase of primitive accumulation in which various strata of surplus populations are created. If left to their own devices, the unemployed and underemployed poor can constitute dangerous classes from the perspective of the forces of order.

All the forms of our internment and enlistment in the security regime, in fact, fulfill the role that Marx credits to the "bloody legislation" in precapitalist England directed at the propertyless and vagrant classes. In addition to coercing the formerly rural populations to accept sedentary jobs in urban centers, the legislation also created the discipline by which the future proletarians would accept wage labor as if it were their own wish and destiny. So, too, our participation in security society operates as a kind of training or *dressage* of our desires and hopes but also and most importantly our fears. Prison functions in part as a warehouse for surplus population but also as a frightening lesson to the "free" population.

Furthermore, the current economic and financial crisis adds a whole series of other fears. And in many cases one of the greatest fears is that of being out of work and thus not being able to survive. You have to be good worker, loyal to your employer, and not go out on strike, or you'll find yourself out of work and unable to pay your debts.

Fear is the primary motivation for the securitized to accept not only its double role, watcher and watched, in the surveillance regime but also the fact that so many others are even further deprived of their freedom. The securitized lives in fear of a combination of punishments and external threats. Fear of the ruling powers and their police is a factor but more important and effective is fear of dangerous others and unknown threats—a generalized social fear. In some ways those who are in prison have less to fear; rather, even though the threats they face from the carceral machine, the guards, and other inmates, are severe, they are more limited and knowable. Fear in the security regime is an empty signifier in which all kinds of terrifying phantoms can appear.

Thomas Jefferson, in one of his least glorious and least courageous moments, was driven by fear to justify not only the compromise to allow slavery in the new state of Missouri but also the continuation of slavery in the United States. "We have the wolf by the ear," he writes, "and we can neither hold him, nor safely let him go. Justice is in one scale, and self-preservation in the other." Since injustices to generations of black slaves have accumulated in their bones a rightful rage, Jefferson reasons, which, if unleashed, will destroy white society, slavery, although unjust, must be continued in order to hold the beast at bay. Today's securitized society functions by the same ignoble logic but now the wolves are already loose, lurking in the shadows, a perpetual threat. All kinds of injustices can be warranted by the ghostly apparitions of a generalized fear.

The Represented

We are constantly told that we are in the midst of a long historical trajectory from diverse forms of tyranny to democracy.

Even though in some places people are repressed by totalitarian or despotic regimes, representative forms of government, which claim to be both democratic and capitalist, are increasingly widespread. Universal suffrage is valued and practiced, albeit with different levels of effectiveness, throughout the world. The global capitalist market, we are told, always extends the model of parliamentary representation as an instrument of the political inclusion of populations. And yet, many of the movements of 2011 refuse to be represented and direct their strongest critiques against the structures of representative government. How can they heap abuse on the precious gift of representation that modernity has bequeathed them? Do they want to return to the dark ages of nonrepresentative government and tyranny? No, of course not. To understand their critique we must recognize that representation is not, in fact, a vehicle of democracy but instead an obstacle to its realization, and we must see how the figure of *the represented* gathers together the figures of the indebted, the mediatized, and the securitized, and at the same time, epitomizes the end result of their subordination and corruption.

The power of finance and wealth, first of all, takes away the possibility for people to associate and construct organizations able to sustain the ever-higher costs of electoral campaigns. Only if you are rich, very rich, can you enter the field on your own resources. Otherwise, to reach the same goal, it is necessary to corrupt and be corrupted. When in government, elected representatives further enrich themselves. Second, what truths can ever be politically constructed if one doesn't control powerful media? Lobbies and capitalist financing campaigns are extremely effective in shepherding into office the political castes that dominate us. The symbolic overdetermination of the dominant media always contains—and often blocks—the social developments of independent struggles, popular alliances, and the dialectic between movements and governments. In short, the dominant media create obstacles to every emergent form of democratic participation. Third, the fear of the securitized is produced in an insidious and lurid way by the scare tactics of the dominant media. Watching the evening news is enough to make you afraid to go outside: reports of children kidnapped from supermarket isles, terrorist bombing plots, psycho-killers in the neighborhood, and more. The associative nature of social relations is transformed into a fearful isolation. *Homo homini lupus est*: to other men, man is a dangerous wolf. Original sin is perpetually present, and fanaticism and violence constantly generate, often for a fee, scapegoats and pogroms against minorities and alternative ideas. Through the processes of representation, politics dumps this world of filth on the represented.

In the modern bourgeois society of the twentieth century, the citizen, as well as the exploited and the alienated (including the disciplined working class), still had some avenues for political action through the (often corporatist) institutions of the state and civil society. Participation in trade unions, political parties, and more generally the associations of civil society opened some spaces for political life. For many people the nostalgia for those times is strong but is often based on hypocritical attachments. How rapidly have we witnessed the withering and extinction of that civil society! Today the structures of participation are invisible (often criminal or simply controlled by lobbies, as we said), and the represented acts in a society bereft of intelligence and manipulated by the deafening imbecility of the media circus, suffering the opacity of information as an absence of virtue and registering only the cynical transparency of the power of the wealthy made more vulgar by a lack of responsibility.

The represented recognizes the collapse of the structures of representation but sees no alternative and is thrust back into fear. From this fear arise populist or charismatic forms of a politics emptied of even the pretense of representation. The extinction of civil society and its broad fabric of institutions was in part the effect of the decline of the social presence of the working class, its organizations, and its unions. It was also due to a blinding of the hope of transformation or, really, a suicide of entrepreneurial capacities, liquefied by the hegemony of financial capital and the exclusive value of rent as a mechanism for social cohesion. Social mobility in these societies becomes, especially for those who in the past were called *bourgeois* (then middle class and now often confused in the crisis with strata of the proletariat), a descent into a dark, bottomless hole. Fear dominates. Thus come charismatic leaders to protect these classes and populist organizations to convince them they belong to an identity, which is merely a social grouping that is no longer coherent.

But even if everything were to function as it should and political representation were characterized by transparency and perfection, representation is in itself, by definition, a mechanism that separates the population from power, the commanded from those who command. When the eighteenth-century republican constitutions were drafted and representation was configured as the center of the rising political order (as sovereign subject, par excellence), it was already clear that political representation did not function through an effective participation of the population, even those white male subjects who were designated as "the people." It was rather conceived as a "relative" democracy, in the sense that representation functioned, at once, to connect the people to and separate them from the structures of power.

Jean-Jacques Rousseau theorized the social contract (and thus the foundation of modern democracy) in these terms: a political system must be invented that can guarantee democracy in a situation in which private property generates inequality and thus puts freedom in danger, a system that can construct a state, defend private property, and define public property as something that, belonging to everyone, belongs to no one. Representation would thus be at the service of all but, being of all, would be of no one. For Rousseau, representation is generated by a (metaphysical) passage from the "will of all" that constitutes society to the "general will," that is, the will of those preselected by all but who respond to none. As Carl Schmitt says, to represent means to make present an absence or, really, a no one. Schmitt's conclusion is perfectly coherent with Rousseau's presuppositions, which themselves are expressed in the US Constitution and the constitutions of the French Revolution. The paradox of representation is complete. It is surprising only that it could function for so long and, in its emptiness, could only have done so supported by the will of the powerful, the possessors of wealth, the producers of information, and the solicitors of fear, preaching superstition and violence.

Today, however, even if we were to believe the modern myths of representation and accept it as a vehicle of democracy, the political context that makes it possible has radically diminished. Since systems of representation were constructed primarily on the national level, the emergence of a global power structure dramatically undermines them. The emerging global institutions make little pretense to represent the will of populations. Policy accords are agreed on and business contracts are signed and guaranteed within the structures of global governance, outside of any representative capacity of the nation-states. Whether there exist "constitutions without states," the function of representation that, in a mystified way, pretended to put the people in power is surely no longer effective in this global terrain.

And the represented? What remains of its qualities as citizen in this global context? No longer an active participant in political life, the represented finds itself poor among the poor, fighting in the jungle of this social life, alone. If it does not rouse its vital senses and awaken its appetite for democracy, it will become a pure product of power, the empty shell of a mechanism of governance that no longer makes reference to the citizen-worker. The represented, then, like the other figures, is the product of mystification. Just as the indebted is denied control of its productive social power; just as the intelligence, affective capacities, and powers of linguistic invention of the mediatized are betrayed; and just as the securitized, living in a world reduced to fear and terror, is deprived of every possibility of associative, just, and loving social exchange, so, too, does the represented have no access to effective political action.

So many of the movements of 2011 direct their critiques against political structures and forms of representation, then, because they recognize clearly that representation, even when it is effective, blocks democracy rather than fosters it. Where, they ask, has the project for democracy gone? How can we engage it again? What does it mean to win back (or, really, to realize for the first time) the political power of the citizen-worker?

One path, the movements teach, passes through the revolt and rebellion against the impoverished and depotentialized subjective figures we have outlined in this chapter. Democracy will be realized only when a subject capable of grasping and enacting it has emerged.

Chapter 2: Rebellion against the Crisis

Today's neoliberal leaders—from their government offices and corporate boardrooms, their media outlets and stock exchange floors—constantly repeat to us that the crisis is dire and our situation is desperate. We are on the *Titanic*, they tell us, and if we want to be saved from the ultimate catastrophe, we have to agree to worsen even further the situation of the indebted, the mediatized, the securitized, and the represented. They promise us that making things worse is our only salvation! Isn't it possible to rise up and give voice to the indignation that seethes in all of us when faced with this blackmail?

All four of the dominated figures of contemporary society have the capacity to rebel and also to invert themselves and become figures of power. This inversion is the result not of a dialectical process but of an event, a subjective *kairos* that breaks the relations of domination and overthrows the processes that reproduce the figures of subjugation. This is not just theoretical conjecture on our part, but rather a reality supported and confirmed by the cycle of struggles that began in 2011, which construct a series of instances of rebellion and resistance.

The neoliberal transformations of social, economic, and political life have not simply disempowered and impoverished the subjects they have produced. The impoverishment that today's proletariat undergoes is not only, in fact, as Marx and Friedrich Engels theorized, a lowering of wages and an exhaustion of the material resources of individual and collective life but also (and increasingly) the deprivation of our human capabilities, especially our capacity for political action. Hannah Arendt, for one, well grasped and anticipated, in the era of triumphant capitalism, this generalized reduction of the potential of human action. By following the recent phenomena we have been describing, in fact, she could have deepened her understanding of this process and her concept of *action*. This concept is not only different from the heavy and deadening aspects of exploited and bureaucratized labor in the capitalist era, but it can also be a living *kairos* that traverses and subverts those conditions of work and exploitation, a *kairos* of resistance.

When you bend under the weight of debt, when your attention is hypnotically glued to your screen, when you have made your house into a prison, you realize how much the capitalist crisis individualizes and strains the human passions. You are alone, depotentialized. But as soon as you look around, you see that the crisis has also resulted in a being together. In the crisis, indebtedness, mediatization, securitization, and representation designate a collective condition. There is no alternative, certainly; we are on the decks of the *Titanic*, and this impoverishment and reduction of the power of singularities make our life into a gray indifference. But we are here together. There is a *kairos* of resistance as well as a *kairos* of community.

We must struggle to liberate ourselves from these conditions of impoverishment, misery, and solitude. But how can we begin? The depotentialized subject is a figure that has been separated from what it can do, as Deleuze says in his reading of Nietzsche:

"Une force séparée de ce qu'elle peut." We must discover a force that reconnects action to being together. Indignation, for example, which expresses individual suffering, alludes even in its solitary resistance to being together. It becomes singular, because becoming singular, in contrast to becoming individual, means finding once again the subjective force in being together. A singular subjectivity discovers that there is no event without a recomposition with other singularities, that there is no being together of singular subjectivities without rebellion. A process of singularization is thus incarnated: a self-affirmation, a self-valorization, and a subjective decision that all open toward a state of being together. All political movements are born this way: from a decision of rupture to a proposition of acting together.

Invert the Debt

The process of subjectivation begins with refusal. I won't. We won't pay *your* debt. We refuse to be evicted from our houses. We will not submit to austerity measures. Instead we want to appropriate your—or, really, *our*—wealth.

In certain periods, when the crisis strikes with its hardest blows, for instance, which individuals have to withstand alone, the will to resist arises with extreme and desperate force. Where does it come from? Many philosophers locate the origin of the will in lack, as if in order to want or act one must be focused on what is missing. But that's not true. The will is born positively from the impulse to affirm a plenitude not a lack, the urge to develop a desire. The will not to pay debts means not only seeking what we don't have, what has been lost, but also and more importantly affirming and developing what we desire, what is better and more beautiful: the sociality and the fullness of social relationships.

The refusal of debt, therefore, does not mean breaking social ties and legal relationships to create an empty, individualized, fragmented terrain. We flee those bonds and those debts in order to give new meaning to the terms *bond* and *debt*, and to discover new social relationships. Marx was being realistic when he spoke about money as the primary social connection in capitalist society. "The individual," he wrote, "carries his social power, as well as his bond with society, in his pocket." The refusal of debt aims to destroy the power of money and the bonds it creates and simultaneously to construct new bonds and new forms of debt. We become increasingly indebted to one another, linked not by financial bonds but by social bonds.

The subjective figures characterized by this social interdependence have already been prepared and developed in the new economic situation, hegemonized by biopolitical production, by a life invested by valorization, and founded on the cooperation of singularities. Cooperation and productive interdependence are the conditions of the common, and the common is now what constitutes the primary basis of social production. Our social bonds, which link us to one another, become a means of production. In our interdependence, in our commonality, we discover productivity and power.

This is why, even though the flows of financial debt have individualizing effects (along with suffering, desperation, and pain—all of which are doubled by our isolation), the new forms of debt become ever more social and anti-individual, transitive, and singular rather than closed in a contractual relationship. When the subject reaches this awareness, when the singularity exits from the spirals of disempowerment and impoverishment to which it was subjected, then it can see that these social bonds and social debts cannot be measured, or better, that they cannot be measured in traditional, quantitative terms. They can be given only in qualitative terms, as vehicles of desire, as decisions to pull ourselves out of the old misery and break the old ties of debt.

The social forms of debt that result demonstrate the virtuous side of the common. These are debts, first of all, for which there is no creditor, and these debts are defined by binding relationships among singularities. Further, they are not bound by morality and guilt. Instead of moral obligation, they function through an ethics of the common, based on the reciprocal recognition of the social debts we owe to one another and to society.

In recent decades numerous struggles of the poor and the impoverished have been waged against the individual and collective yoke of debt. Occupy Wall Street may be the most visible example, since Wall Street serves as the ultimate symbol of the global debt society, the metonym for all creditors, but those protests by no means stand alone. We see two primary streams of recent debt protests that feed into the encampments at Zuccotti Park. One stream, which concentrates primarily on the sovereign debt of subordinated countries, stretches back through the various alterglobalization protests against the World Bank and IMF to its pinnacle in the 2001 Argentina popular uprising and assembly movement against the neoliberal politics of economic crisis, which was preceded by the dozens of "IMF riots" against austerity programs from 1989 in Venezuela to 1977 in Egypt and 1976 in Peru. The other stream, which is more fractured, is characterized by protests against the burdens of individual and individualizing debts on the poor, such as the riots in Los Angeles in 1992, Paris in 2005, and London in 2011. These three riots were all expressions of rage against racial subordination in the metropolis, and they were all set off by acts of police violence, but the racial character was powerfully crossed in each case with the refusal of the power of commodities and wealth. Looting and burning were fueled, in part, by a desire for the commodities that have been denied, but the events were also a symbolic destruction of the ways in which those commodities serve as vehicles of social subordination.

We know that some are reluctant to group together the orderly occupiers of Zuccotti Park and even the carnivalesque alterglobalization protesters with the poor and impoverished rioters' savage jacqueries and violent expressions of rage. Don't think, though, that some of these struggles are more advanced and others more backward. No, the old Bolshevik theory of a passage of political consciousness from spontaneity to organization no longer has a place here. And let's have no moralizing about how the rebellions of the poor should be better organized, more constructive, and less violent. On US college campuses the police use pepper spray, whereas in the dark sections of the metropolis they shoot with live rounds. What is most important in each of these struggles, we think, is to understand how the powerful refusals, expressed in various ways, are accompanied by processes capable of forming new social bonds. They do not seek to restore an order and they do not ask for justice or reparations for the offended, but they want instead to construct another possible world.

Make the Truth

When we refuse to be mediatized, we have not only to stop allowing ourselves to be fooled, believing everything we read in the papers, and simply digesting the truths we are fed, but also we need to break our attention away from the media. It sometimes seems that we are enthralled to video screens and can't take our eyes off them. How often have you seen people walking (and even driving!) on city streets with their heads down while texting who then bump into each other as if hypnotized? Break the spell and discover a new way to communicate! It is not only or even primarily that we need different information or different technologies. Yes, we need to discover the truth, but also, and more important, we need to make new truths, which can be created only by singularities in networks communicating and being together.

Political projects that focus on providing information, although certainly important, can easily lead to disappointment and disillusionment. If only the people of the United States knew what their government is doing and the crimes it has committed, one might think, they would rise up and change it. But, in fact, even if they were to read all the books by Noam Chomsky and all the material released by WikiLeaks, they could still vote the same politicians back in power and, ultimately, reproduce the same society. Information alone is not enough. The same is true of practices of ideology critique, more generally: revealing the truth about power does not stop people from striving for their servitude as if it were their liberation. And neither is it enough to open a space for communicative action in the public sphere. The mediatized is not a figure of false consciousness but rather one caught in the web, attentive, enthralled.

Before you can *actively* communicate in networks, you must become a singularity. The old cultural projects against alienation wanted you to return to yourself. They battled the ways in which capitalist society and ideology have separated us from

ourselves, broken us in two, and thus sought a form of whole-
ness and authenticity, most often in individual terms. When
you become a singularity, instead, you will never be a whole
self. Singularities are defined by being multiple internally and
finding themselves externally only in relation to others. The
communication and expression of singularities in networks,
then, is not individual but choral, and it is always operative,
linked to a doing, making ourselves while being together.

When we become unmediatized we don't cease to interact
with media—indeed the movements of 2011 are known for
their employment of social media such as Facebook and Twitter—but our relationship to media changes. First, as singularities we gain a free mobility in networks. We swarm like insects,
follow new pathways, and come together in new patterns and
constellations. The form of political organization is central
here: a decentralized multitude of singularities communicates
horizontally (and social media are useful to them because they
correspond to their organizational form). Demonstrations and
political actions are born today not from a central committee
that gives the word but rather from the coming together of and
the discussion among numerous small groups. After the
demonstration, similarly, messages spread virally through the
neighborhoods and a variety of metropolitan circuits.

Second, media become tools for our collective self-produc-
tion. We are able to create new truths only when we cease to
be individual and constitute ourselves in our relationships to
others, opening ourselves to a common language. Making the
truth is a collective linguistic act of creativity. Sometimes the
creation and diffusion of political slogans in demonstrations
constitute an act of truth making. The discourse of the 99 percent versus the 1 percent that emerged from the Occupy move-

ments, for example, illuminated the reality of social inequality and dramatically shifted the terms of public debate. A more complex example is the truth created by the 2001 Argentine slogan, "Que se vayan todos" ("Throw them all out"). The slogan expressed in condensed form not only the corruption of politicians, political parties, and the constitutional system itself, but also the potential for a new, participatory democracy. Such productions of truth also involve the creation of political affects by negotiating the terms of our being together in relation to each other. Expressing these political affects in being together embodies a new truth.

Real communication among singularities in networks thus requires an encampment. This is the kind of self-learning experience and knowledge production that takes place, for example, in student occupations. The moment feels magical and enlightening because in being together a collective intelligence and a new kind of communication are constructed. In the occupied squares of 2011, from Tahrir to Puerta del Sol to Zuccotti Park, new truths were produced through discussion, conflict, and consensus in assemblies. Working groups and commissions on topics from housing rights and mortgage foreclosures to gender relations and violence function as both self-learning experiences and means to spread knowledge production. Anyone who has lived through such an encampment recognizes how new knowledges *and* new political affects are created in the corporeal and intellectual intensity of the interactions.

The clearest contemporary example of the communicative capacity of an encampment is perhaps the decades-long experiment of the Zapatista self-rule in Chiapas, Mexico. The EZLN was renowned early in its existence for its novel use of the

media, including electronic communiqués and Internet post-
ings from the Lacandon jungle. Even more important and innovative, though, are the communicative networks and political
truths created in the Zapatista community practices of collective self-government. Constant attempts in the communities
to subvert gender and social hierarchies and to open to all decision-making and governing responsibilities give substance
and meaning to their projects to lead by following and to walk
forward questioning.

Break Free

Of all the ways that people refuse the security regime today,
the most significant are modalities of flight. You can't beat the
prison, and you can't fight the army. All you can do is flee. Break
your chains and run. Most often, flight involves not coming out
into the open but rather becoming invisible. Since security
functions so often by making you visible, you have to escape
by refusing to be seen. Becoming invisible, too, is a kind of
flight. The fugitive, the deserter, and the invisible are the real
heroes (or antiheroes) of the struggle of the securitized to be
free. But when you run, think of George Jackson and grab a
weapon as you go. It might come in handy down the road.

You are only able really to refuse and flee, though, when you
recognize your power. Those living under the weight of a security regime tend to think of themselves as powerless, dwarfed
by against its overarching might. Those in a prison society think
of themselves as living in the belly of a Leviathan, consumed
by its power. How can we possibly match its firepower, how
can we escape its all-seeing eyes and its all-knowing information systems? To find a way out all you have to do is remember
the basic recognition of the nature of power explained by Fou-

cault and, before him, Niccolò Machiavelli: power is not a thing but a relation. No matter how mighty and arrogant seems that power standing above you, know that it depends on you, feeds on your fear, and survives only because of your willingness to participate in the relationship. Look for an escape door. One is always there. Desertion and disobedience are reliable weapons against voluntary servitude.

Sometimes flight takes unusual forms. The Marranos in fifteenth-century Spain, for instance, were forced to convert to Christianity but continued to practice Judaism in secret. They led a double life: obeying when the forces of power were watching and subverting that power in hidden spaces. They conducted a kind of secret flight while staying still.

Part of our fight has to be not only against the ubiquitous tentacles of the security system, but also against the very real and concrete walls of the prison and the military barracks. Angela Davis, for instance, rightly calls for the abolition of the prison. Given the racial composition of prisons in the United States (and immigration detention centers everywhere), the struggle against the prison today is the core of a new abolitionism, putting an end to some of the most extreme structures of racial segregation and subordination. Today's prisons clearly have none of the noble functions of reeducation or social reintegration that nineteenth-century reformers imagined. On the contrary, prison is a machine that creates and re-creates antisocial subjectivities, perpetuates fear, and poisons social relations.

The struggle against the military and militarization is equally important. The warnings of an illustrious catalog of US presidents that military establishments undermine public freedom and democracy have gone almost entirely unheeded: from

Thomas Jefferson's and James Madison's polemics against standing armies to Dwight D. Eisenhower's somber premonition of the disasters resulting from the collusion of an immense military establishment and powerful weapons industries. For a nation that so venerates its founding fathers and past presidents, the United States is remarkably deaf to their pleadings on this subject. Like prisons, militaries degrade subjectivities and poison social relations. Not only are returning soldiers damaged by war and hierarchy, but they spread their diseased subjectivities among the families they return to and everyone with whom they interact. Feminists have long analyzed the power, fragility, and pathologies of the forms of masculinity propagated and reproduced by militarism.

Projects for the abolition of the prison and the military are just and have important positive effects, but one should recognize that these struggles are impossible to realize fully in our societies as they are currently structured. The prison and the military are poisons, but perversely, the sick body must keep ingesting them to survive, making itself constantly worse. Prison creates a society that needs prisons, and the military creates a society that needs militarism. Going cold turkey would be suicide. The body must be cured instead over an extended period to purge itself of the poison.

The key to a healthy society is to put an end to fear and thus to create real freedom and security. One of the most moving and inspiring scenes from Cairo's Tahrir Square in February 2011, only days after pro-government forces had rampaged through the square on horses and camels, brutally beating protesters. Instead of decrying the injustice or affirming how they would defend themselves in the future, people began to say, simply and remarkably, "We are not afraid anymore." This pulled out the crucial block that held up the Mubarak regime. Three months later in Madrid's Puerta del Sol, when the encampments were threatened by police, their response echoed the affirmations from Egypt, "No tenemos miedo." We can't fully explain how these militants achieved such a state of fearlessness, which must have been due in large part to their being together in the square, but we can easily recognize its political power and importance. Power cannot survive when its subjects free themselves from fear.

Such expressions of fearlessness might bring to mind the revolutionary heroism of a Che Guevara, the warrior who goes willingly to his death with confidence that the greater cause will continue. We have little interest, though, in heroes and martyrs. Moreover, we think the ability of those encamped in these squares to shake off fear has little to do with heroism or even death. "A free man," Spinoza proclaims rather cryptically, "thinks of death least of all, and his wisdom is a meditation on life, not death." Real security, in Spinoza's view, does not result from accumulating the most power so as to overwhelm all enemies, nor does it require fending off death or holding evil at bay, like Saint Paul's *katechon*. We have no illusions about immortality, but we are so focused on the joys of life that death becomes an afterthought. The encamped protesters—being together, discussing, disagreeing, struggling—seem to have rediscovered a truth that Spinoza foresaw: real security and the destruction of fear can be achieved only through the collective construction of freedom.

Constitute Yourself

You don't represent me! ¡*Que se vayan todos*! Such refusals of representation and representative governmental structures have been pronounced by millions during the crisis of neoliberalism at the beginning of the twenty-first century. One novelty of these protests and these refusals consists in the fact that they immediately make clear that the crisis is not only economic, social, and political, but also constitutional. Representative structures and liberal governance regimes are all thrown into question. The audacious conceptual leap made by the theory and practice of parliamentary representation (from the "will of all" to the "general will") has finally proven to be fatal, and even the new forms of governance pulled out as a safety net to catch the falling acrobat have proven too weak and frayed. It's increasingly hard for anyone to believe in the resurrection and redemption of the constitution. *Ancien régime* was once the name for the rule of those in powdered wigs, but now instead the representative machine is an ancien régime! The republican constitutions have had their time, more than two centuries. Isn't that enough?

Political and constitutional debate has to be reopened. And the radical change demanded today is not only about content (from the private and the public to the common) but also about form. How can people associate closely together in the common and participate directly in democratic decision making? How can the multitude become prince of the institutions of the common in a way that reinvents and realizes democracy? This is the task of a constituent process.

When financial debts have been transformed into social bonds, when singularities interact in productive networks, and when the desire for security is freed from fear, then, from the inversion of these three figures, subjectivities capable of democratic action will begin to emerge. In the bourgeois societies of the industrial era, the available avenues for political action were primarily corporatist and individualist; in postindustrial, neoliberal societies, the possibilities are even more meager, and the represented is allowed only a passive and generic political role. The movement from the bourgeois citizen to the represented was universalizing in its juridical form and yet gradually emptied of any content. Now new figures of political subjectivity can instead discover forms of participation that overflow corporatist and individualist divisions, and that give substance and content to the generic and abstract forms of political activity. The mechanisms of the production of rules can be constructed only in singular form according to common modalities. From now on constituent powers must function and be continually renewed from below.

But why, some friends ask us, are we still taking about constitutions? Why can't we free ourselves from all normative structures and institutions? Every revolution needs a constituent power—not to bring the revolution to an end but to continue it, guarantee its achievements, and keep it open to further innovations. A constituent power is necessary to organize social production and social life in accordance with our principles of freedom, equality, and solidarity. Constituent processes constantly revise political structures and institutions to be more adequate to the social fabric and material foundation of social conflicts, needs, and desires.

Said more philosophically, constituent processes are *dispositifs* of the production of subjectivity. But why, our friends repeat, must subjectivities be produced? Why can't we just be ourselves? Because even if there were some original or primordial human nature to be expressed, there is no reason to believe it would foster free, equal, and democratic social and political relations. Political organization always requires the production of subjectivities. We must create a multitude capable of democratic political action and the self-management of the common.

An example can help clarify one aspect of this proposition. When the Spanish *indignados*, who had occupied the squares in the spring of 2011, refused to participate in the fall 2011 national elections, they were strongly criticized. Their detractors called them impotent anarchists and called their refusal to engage with state institutions and electoral politics ideological and hysterical. They were breaking apart the Left! The *indignados*, of course, are not anarchists, and they are not responsible for fragmenting the Left. Instead they have created a rare opportunity for reforming and relaunching a new and different Left. A few years earlier many of them were the same activists who, when right-wing politicians publicly attributed the tragic bombing at Madrid's Atocha train station to Basque militants, immediately proclaimed the truth through an extraordinary relay on cell phones and other media—*pásalo*, they wrote, "pass it on"—and their actions effectively ushered the socialists and Zapatero to a surprise electoral victory. The *indignados* did not participate in the 2011 elections, then, in part because they refused to reward a socialist party that had continued neoliberal policies and betrayed them during its years in office, but also and more importantly because they now have larger battles to fight, in particular one aimed at the structures of representation and the constitutional order itself—a fight whose Spanish roots reach back to the tradition of antifascist struggles and throw a new and critical light on the so-called transition to democracy that followed the end of the Franco regime. The *indignados* think of this as a *destituent* rather than a *constituent* process, a kind of exodus from the existing political structures, but it is necessary to prepare the basis for a new constituent power.

Chapter 3: Constituting the Common

Declaration of Principles

In the previous chapters, we insisted on the fact that neoliberal capitalism fails to produce, sustain, and guarantee effective rules of global governance, and consequently, the financial markets are continually able to overwhelm economies and societies in such a way that further disadvantages the poor. Two additional characteristics define the current situation. First, as we have argued extensively elsewhere, production is now realized at both the local and global levels in the frame of the common: labor power has become common, life has been put to work, capitalist development in the form of financialization centrally involves exploitation of the common, and so forth. Second, capitalist development is plagued by an irresolvable economic, social, and political crisis. This crisis can be explained in part, at least, by the fact that whereas productive forces are becoming increasingly common, relations of production and property continue to be defined by individualistic and privatistic rules and norms, which are unable to grasp the new productive reality and are completely external to the new common sources of value.

It is clear, however, that, in contrast to governments in the 1930s in the face of crises of similar intensity, today's ruling powers are incapable of developing a political solution adequate to the depth of the economic and social predicament. No John Maynard Keynes or Franklin D. Roosevelt has emerged on the scene, and their old recipes, which had some validity for the industrial production of their time, cannot be adapted to our postindustrial era. The ruling neoliberal, market-based policy frameworks have nothing to propose. What we need instead is a qualitative leap, a paradigm shift.

The ruling powers are also unable to propose a constitutional reform that would address the crisis. The modern history of constitutional reform has always involved constructed mediations, which regarded, first, in the case of liberal constitutions, the mercantile relations of exchange and, later, in the case of welfarist constitutions, a dialectic between capital and labor. It is difficult to imagine today what mediations could be constructed regarding the processes of financialization that live at the heart of the contemporary economy. Categories such as representation and democracy, let alone national sovereignty, cannot be redefined without recognizing that global financial markets have become the preeminent seat of the autonomous production of legality and politics. The command exercised by finance tends increasingly to leap over the institutional mediations of the nation-states and impose a kind of blackmail by which not only employment and salaries but also the enjoyment of basic rights (from housing to health) depend ineluctably on the dynamics and fluctuations of financial markets.

And yet, in this situation, numerous political struggles, especially the encampments of 2011, have put forward new principles that have great constitutional relevance. They have made of these principles a new common sense and designated them as the basis of a project of constituent action. Believing that only a constituent process based in the common can provide a real alternative, we thus hold these truths to be self-evident, that all people are equal, that they have acquired through political struggle certain inalienable rights, that among these are not only life, liberty, and the pursuit of happiness but also free access to the common, equality in the distribution of wealth, and the sustainability of the common. It is equally evident that to secure these rights, democratic governance must be instituted, deriving its just powers from the participation of the governed and the transparency of governmental organization. It is evident, finally, that whenever any form of government becomes destructive of these ends, it is the right of the people to alter or to abolish it and to institute new government, laying its foundation on such principles and organizing its powers in such form as to them shall seem most likely to affect their safety and happiness.

Constituent Struggles

We consider to be *constituent* the struggles that are posed on the terrain of the common and that not only express the urgent need but also chart the path for a new constitutional process. Some of the French and American founding fathers, most notably Nicolas de Condorcet and Thomas Jefferson, advocated that each generation must create its own constitution. In line with that principle, today we must grasp the dramatic break that is determined between the existing constitutional institutions and the democratic needs that common sense demands. When a long train of abuses and usurpations, as the tradition teaches us, pursuing invariably the same object evinces a design to reduce them under absolute despotism, it is our right, it is our duty, to throw off such government and to provide new guards for our future security. Today's struggles thus present, first of all, destituent rather than constituent characteristics. They must destroy the despotic effects left in us and our societies through the exhaustion of the old constitutions.

The new struggles thus present a profound asymmetry with what we can now call the ancien régime. Foucault insists that power is always an action of one subject on another and that power is thus always a relationship between command and resistance. But when the movements develop with such intensity, they often break away from preexisting relations and find themselves, at that point, already on the other side. A declaration of independence creates the real basis for a new constituent process. The struggles express today, in other words, the contingent result of political conflicts as well as an event, an overflowing of desire and political proposition. The common sense that dwells in the hearts and heads of the subjects who conduct the struggles and imagine a new society has a prescriptive value and the power to generate, animate, and regulate new forms of life. Declaring their independence from the ancien régime, they root themselves in a new ontological condition and establish the circumstances under which more equal, common, and sustainable relations can grow. This constituent power is deeply embedded in the struggles, and these declarations of inalienable rights reveal the course of a historical movement that is reaching its maturity.

The fact that such constituent struggles can fail in the short term does not derail this process. We have witnessed extraordinary movements that inflamed North Africa, as well as several countries in the Middle East and the Arabian Peninsula. Some of these, in the spring of 2011, achieved swift success, overthrowing corrupt governments and business cliques that had dominated with tyrannical powers and the aid of former colonial masters. But in all the countries that entered into struggle, including those where reactionary forces blocked the way and those in which democratic movements won initial victories, the political situation has in one way or another been led back into the hands of conservative elites. Does this mean, then, that the constituent struggles were useless? Of course not. Inalienable principles of freedom and equality were affirmed in that spring that may take more time to be realized fully. And, furthermore, those principles traveled from North Africa to Spain, Greece, the United States, and elsewhere. The struggles have expressed new rights in an insurrectional way, have made new constitutional powers emerge that, although now latent, maintain pressure and have stripped the veil from ignorance and domination, obedience and fear. From now on, in every year there will be a springtime of nature as well as one of politics.

Autonomous time. When we insist on the long and expansive temporality of the Arab spring it might seem that we are introducing surreptitiously a conception of time different from the insurrectional acceleration of events that seemed to define the beginnings of those struggles. The process of decision making in open, horizontal assemblies, which characterized all the encampments of 2011, is also often extraordinarily slow. Should the slow time and *longue durée* of institutional processes thus be privileged over insurrectional events, as Alexis de Tocqueville suggested long ago? No, we don't think so. What is interesting and new in these struggles is not so

much their slowness or swiftness, but rather the political autonomy by which they manage their time. This marks an enormous difference from the rigid and exhausting rhythms of the
alterglobalization movements that followed the schedule of
summit meetings early in the new century. Instead, in the 2011
cycle of struggles, speed, slowness, deep intensities, and superficial accelerations are combined and mixed. In every instance, time is withdrawn from the schedule imposed by
external pressures and electoral seasons, establishing its own
calendar and rhythms of development.

The notion of an autonomous temporality helps us clarify
what we mean when we claim that these movements present
an *alternative*. An alternative is not an action, a proposition, or
a discourse that is simply opposed to the program of power, but
rather it is a new *dispositif* that is based in a radically asymmet-
rical standpoint. This standpoint is *elsewhere* even when it
shares the same space. Its autonomy makes coherent the
rhythms of its temporality, as well as its production of subjectivities, struggles, and constituent principles.

The temporal determinations of constituent action fluctuate
between dormancy and rapidity in relation to other factors as
well. Most important, perhaps, is how every constituent action
is contagious and infectious. Demanding freedom in the face
of a dictatorial power, for example, also introduces and spreads
the idea of the equal distribution of wealth, as in Tunisia and
Egypt; posing the desire for democracy against traditional political structures of representation also raises the need for participation and transparency, as in Spain; protesting the
inequalities created by financial control also leads to demands
for the democratic organization of and free access to the common, as in the United States; and so forth. Our primary interest

here is not to follow the logical sequences of each political and constitutional claim but rather to describe or make felt the movements created in the spread of these constituent instances and in the different revolutionary occasions. Temporalities are swift or slow according to the viral intensity of the communication of ideas and desires, which institute in each case a singular synthesis.

The slow temporality of constituent movements—typified by the deliberation of the assemblies—allows for and requires the spread and expression (as well as the control) of knowledges and expertise. If there ever existed an "autonomy of the political" à la Schmitt, you certainly won't find it here. The constituent decisions of the encampments are formed through a complex construction and negotiation of knowledges and will, which takes time. No single leader or central committee decides. The often slow and complex decision-making procedures, supported by widespread knowledge and expertise, also mark a significant element of the anthropological (or ontological) difference of the new constituent movements. The Spanish *indignados* and the occupiers of Wall Street offer powerful examples of this complexity, in the way they combine in discourse and action the critique of the current forms of political life (representation, electoral methods, and so forth), the protest against social inequality, and the attack on financial domination.

Finally, the alternative temporality of these constituent processes fosters both the creation and spread of knowledges as well as the education of political affects. Tahrir Square, Rothschild Boulevard, the occupied Wisconsin statehouse, and Syntagma Square are all, obviously, characterized by intense affects. Affects are expressed at those sites, but more important, they are produced and trained. For professional politicians, and indeed for anyone who has not spent time in the encampments, it is difficult if not impossible to understand how much these constituent experiences are animated and permeated by flows of affects and indeed great joy. Physical proximity, of course, facilitates the common education of the affects, but also essential are the intense experiences of cooperation, the creation of mutual security in a situation of extreme vulnerability, and the collective deliberation and decision-making processes. The encampments are a great factory for the production of social and democratic affects.

Counterpowers. Constituent work is slow and thoroughgoing—it proceeds on its own clock. But there are some pressing issues that won't wait. What good is a beautiful constituent process when people are suffering now? What if, by the time we create a perfect democratic society, the earth is already degraded beyond repair?

The constituent process must be accompanied by a series of counterpowers that take immediate action in areas of social and environmental need and danger. This double relation of constitutional action is something like the relationship established in the thirteenth century at the foundation of the British legal system when the declaration of the Magna Carta was accompanied by a Charter of the Forest, which, as Peter Linebaugh maintains, deserves much more attention than what historians have given it. Whereas the Magna Carta designates the rights of citizens with respect to the sovereign, the Charter of the Forest establishes their rights to access the common. Access to the forest at that time meant a right to the necessities of life, including fuel and food. Today the constituent process must be accompanied by a similar series of actions to guarantee the rights of life and provide the necessities for a safe, healthy, dignified existence.

One realm of such needs includes dangers facing the environment. The degradation and destruction of plant and animal species and the contamination of the earth and seas continues unabated. The dates by which scientists predict a point of no return regarding climate change grow ever closer while carbon dioxide emissions continue to rise—and, shamefully, discussions of those in power shift from strategies of prevention to those of adaptation to a changed climate. Oil spills, radiation leaks, water contamination from processing tar sands—the list of catastrophes grows and the methods of protection have only been weakened in the context of economic crisis, as if concern for the well-being of the earth were an optional concern only for flush times rather than a real necessity for the lives of humans and others. The great corporations, it's probably no surprise, show no ability or willingness to stop their practices of environmental destruction. National governments and supranational institutions, however, have proven equally unable to address the large problems—they are not even able to arrive at agreements, let alone enforce them. It seems that humanity is completely powerless to stop itself from destroying the planet and the necessary conditions for its own life.

Another realm where counterpowers are needed, and which is inextricably related to the environmental concerns, regards the human necessities for food, health, and shelter, which can be addressed in part through access to the common. Housing is an urgent need for people throughout the world. In subordinated countries the lack of housing and substandard housing is often addressed by movements to occupy unused land and structures and to regularize people's right to stay there. In the dominant parts of the world, the economic crisis has led to a rash of foreclosures for people who cannot pay the mortgages owned on their houses or cannot continue to pay the rent. Anti-eviction campaigns must accompany projects for finding adequate housing for those without it. Access to healthy food and water is similarly a need, most pressing in the poorest regions of the world but also real and urgent in the richest. Battles against the privatization of resources such as water are essential.

Environmental and social crises are all exacerbated, furthermore, by innumerable wars that continue across the globe, destroying lives and landscapes. We seem to have entered a stage of history in which the state of war is never-ending, shifting from high to low intensity and back again. The global security regime under which we live does not establish a state of peace but rather makes permanent a war society, with suspensions of rights, elevated surveillance, and the enlistment of all in the war effort. Who will put an end to the wars and the state of war? The dominant nation-states, especially the United States, have certainly not been willing to do so. No one believes at this point in the old ruse of a war to end all wars. Wars only make more and more wars. And even supranational institutions, such as the United Nations, which were born with the dream of peace, have no power to put an end to war.

What kinds of counterpowers can guarantee the continued flourishing of humanity, the animal world, the plant world, and the planet itself? Absolutely essential in this effort is the work that so many are doing today that use the legal means of national and international systems as a kind of counterpower. Class action suits against polluting corporations; human rights demands against war, torture, and police abuse; and advocacy for refugees, migrants, and inmates—these actions use the power of the judge against that of the king, exploiting elements of the legal system against the sovereign power. Although essential, however, the operations of such counterpowers are always limited and circumscribed by the sovereign power to which they appeal, be they nation-states or international systems. Their power is increasingly limited, furthermore, as the sovereign powers of nation-states and international organizations are today progressively eroded.

Biopolitics needs weapons of coercion at its disposal, beyond the means of recourse provided by national and international law, to construct counterpowers. Democratic counterpowers must be able to force the corporations and the nation-states to open access to the common, to divide the wealth equitably so all can meet their basic needs, and to stop the destruction and repair the damage done to social systems and ecosystems, populations and the planet. How can such democratic counterpowers be constructed and where will they get their force? How this will come about is not clear to us. But what is clear are the urgent needs of humanity and the earth, and the incapacities of all the existing powers to fulfill those needs.

All this is a primary preoccupation of those who are in struggle today. Everyone who has even passed through an encampment has wrestled with these problems. And they also have another, more local, and perhaps mundane preoccupation: what does counterpower mean, and what kind of force is adequate when police attack and the forces of order try to evict them? To this, too, we have no satisfying response, only the conviction that the patient constituent processes must be complemented by immediately acting counterpowers.

Communication. One of the protests that proceeded and prepared the terrain for the May 2011 encampments of the *in-*

dignados in Spain expressed opposition to a law proposed by the socialist government (the Sinde law) that threatened to regulate and privatize social networks, as well as criminalizing users. Against the law arose multitudinous encounters and "swarming" uprisings. From the beginning, the objective of the struggle—to liberate networks—also provided its instrument. Liberated networks were, in fact, a primary organizational tool in the Spanish encampments as they had been earlier in the countries on the southern coast of the Mediterranean and as they would be later in the British riots and the Occupy movements. One should always keep together, especially in this case, on one hand, the construction and the circulation of struggles and, on the other, the expressions of constituent power. The immediate themes and instruments of struggle mix in these subversive strategies. The constituent power of the common is thus closely interwoven with the themes of constituent power—adopting new media (cellular technologies, Twitter, Facebook, and more generally the Internet) as vehicles of experimentation with democratic and multitudinary governance.

Issues of communication are immediately intertwined with those of knowledge, today more than ever. We live in a society in which capital functions increasingly by exploiting the production and expression of knowledge, a society of cognitive capitalism. Knowledge ever more constitutes the heart of social relations, in terms of both capitalist control and the resistance of living labor. It is thus no coincidence that, in the current cycle of struggles, a large portion of the activists are students, intellectual workers, and those working in urban service jobs—what some call the cognitive precariat. They mediate on their own skin the activity of communication, intellectual labor, and the efforts required to study. For the Tunisian and Egyptian revolts as much as for those in Spain, Greece, Israel, and the United States, and for those characterized primarily by the call for freedom as much as for those centered on poverty or financial exploitation, this is one solid basis they all share. The proliferation of struggles and their performative character are grounded in the new nature of labor power. As the centrality of cognitive labor becomes hegemonic, it permeates and is crystallized in these forms of struggle. In the passage of these movements from protest to constituent process, then, the demand for the publicity and transparency of power becomes central.

Any effort to discipline or repress the curiosity, vitality, or desire for knowledge of cognitive workers reduces their productivity. These qualities are essential to contemporary economic production, but they also open new contradictions regarding the exercise of power and the legitimacy of representation. In fact, curiosity, vitality, and desire for knowledge demand that the opacity and secrecy of power be destroyed. The figure of the "statesman" itself is under attack and is coming to be considered an indignity. Every form of expertise must be reorganized in the context of plural, widespread political action such that every transcendence of knowledge, just as every transcendence of power, must be eliminated.

One could say, in this regard, that an enormous taboo is being destroyed. For centuries leaders have insisted that democracy and raison d'état go hand in hand. Now, instead, the advent of a real democracy must mean the complete destruction of raison d'état. The activities of WikiLeaks and the anonymous networks that support it, for example, make this abundantly clear. If the state is not willing to initiate a process of Glasnost, opening its secret vaults and making transparent its operations, then these militants will help it do so quickly. This is not just a matter of blowing the whistle on the greatest abuses of power but rather insisting on transparency in the regular functioning of government.

Protection and expression of minorities. The protection of minorities is a classic constitutional conundrum that must be addressed by any schema of majority rule. How can the ruling majority be restrained from oppressing minorities? The classic republican solution is to abrogate majority rule in certain cases by giving representatives the power of decision making. For James Madison, for instance, in *Federalist* 10, the touchstone for legal discussions of the topic, the protection of minorities against the majority is a crucial argument against "pure democracy" and for the rule of representatives. The developments of the movements have shown us, however, that the protection of minorities does not require abrogating majority rule nor does it imply separation in identity groups. Instead, the relationship of singularities in decision-making processes provides mechanisms for the inclusion and expression of differences.

Deciding which minorities to protect in which instances, of course, requires an ethical and political choice. Not all minorities in all instances deserve to be shielded from the majority's decisions. Indeed, most minorities in most cases should be outvoted. Otherwise, majority rule would be meaningless.

Madison gives two primary examples of minorities to be afforded protection, and the difference between them helps clarify this point. The freedom of religious practice of minorities, we certainly agree, should be safeguarded against the domination or coercion of the majority religion. Madison also argues in *Federalist* 10, however, for the protection of the wealthy minority against the poor majority. If not protected, he reasons, the minority of property holders and creditors will be outvoted on economic issues by the majority of the propertyless and the indebted; hence, he fears, the government will have no power to resist the majority's "rage for paper money, for an abolition of debts, for an equal division of property, or for any other improper or wicked project." To protect against such decisions, Madison advocates "the substitution of representatives whose enlightened views and virtuous sentiments" are superior to those of the majority, guaranteeing what such politicians deem to be, to use Rousseau's terms, the general will against the will of all.

Clearly, wealthy property holders and creditors do not need or deserve special protection as a minority beyond the basic protections enjoyed by all. Their wealth already gives them enormous, disproportionate power over the majority. Why should the 1 percent be shielded against the will of the 99 percent in public decision making over economic and social policy? It is bizarre, in fact, that Madison's argument thus puts religious minorities and minorities of powerful, wealthy property holders and creditors on the same level.

How can we guarantee tolerance toward the rights of powerless minorities without conceding decision-making powers to "enlightened" and "virtuous" representatives, as Madison suggests? First of all, we should recognize that contemporary social movements are experimenting with new practices of majority rule that result in new conceptions of tolerance. The movements, for instance, have developed performative practices of expressing the majority will. At different occupations and encampments, in assembly discussions from one hundred to five thousand people, you see people silently wiggling their fingers with hands up or down to express approval or disapproval, respectively, of the speaker. Twitter is similarly used in assemblies for a dynamic expression of majority sentiments. Even though we think such experimentation and novel techniques of expression are important, this is not, for us, the essential point.

More important are the modes of organization of the movements and, specifically, the ways they include differences. Horizontal, democratic assemblies do not expect or seek unanimity but instead are constituted by a plural process that is open to conflicts and contradictions. The decisions of the majority move forward through a process of differential inclusion or, rather, through the agglutination of differences. The work of the assembly, in other words, is to find ways to link different views and different desires such that they can fit together in contingent ways. The majority, then, becomes not a homogeneous unit or even a body of agreement but a concatenation of differences. Minorities are protected, therefore, not by being separated but by being empowered to participate in the process. Such a configuration allows us to leave behind notions of the general will, which rely on the wisdom of representatives, and instead to fashion politics democratically, according to the will of all.

The functioning of such dynamic and internally multiple majorities also transforms the conventional conception of tolerance. Tolerance has often been understood to imply the social separation of minorities and blindness to their difference. You are tolerant of his homosexuality by pretending he is not gay. Or you are tolerant by allowing him to live with others like him, separate from the dominant society. The rule of the majority, however, does not require that minorities be protected either through indifference or by making them an exception and socially separating them. Tolerance must instead give everyone the power to participate *as different* and to work actively with others. This tolerance is an essential feature of the internal multiplicity of the ruling majority.

A plural ontology of politics. The struggles of 2011 we address here took place in sites far apart, and their protagonists have very different forms of life. Some overthrew tyrants and demanded the right to vote in free and fair elections, whereas others criticized and refused political systems of representation; some denounced social and economic inequality and injustice, whereas others destroyed and looted property; some supported and were supported by established labor unions, whereas others concentrated on the precarious workers and the immaterial forms of production that are often not represented by traditional unions; and so forth. Why, then, should we consider these struggles part of the same cycle?

It is true that these struggles confront the same enemy, characterized by the powers of debt, the media, the security regime, and the corrupt systems of political representation. However, the primary point is that their practices, strategies, and objectives, although different, are able to connect and combine with each other to form a plural, shared project. The singularity of each struggle fosters rather than hinders the creation of a common terrain.

Earlier we explained that these movements were born in something like a communicative laboratory, and indeed, the glue that holds them together seems initially to be linguistic, cooperative, and network based (like many forms of cognitive labor). We also noted that this cooperation is constructed in the movements, and their common language is spread widely according to an autonomous temporality, which is often very slow but also self-controlled, self-limiting, and self-managed. The horizontal decision-making processes of the multitude require temporal autonomy. The communication of slogans and militant desires often begins slowly in small community and neighborhood groups, but then at a certain point spreads virally. Some of the Israeli *indignados* camped on Tel Aviv boulevards thought of themselves as renewing the spirit and the political form of the kibbutz tradition, based in such community relationships. Drawing on their antifascist traditions, the Spanish *indignados* demonstrated, in the tents of their encampments and the working groups that developed elements of a political program, how a constituent discourse can—from below and from the simple, local communication of affects, needs, and ideas in urban neighborhoods—rise up to form general assemblies and a decision-making system.

These movements have thus tended to find support and inspiration in federalist models. Small groups and communities find ways to connect with one another and to create common projects not by renouncing but by expressing their differences. Federalism is thus a motor of composition. Clearly, few elements remain here of the theory of the state and federalist sovereignty, but instead at the microlevel reside the passions and intelligence of a federalist logic of association. Many of the weapons deployed against these movements, in fact, are aimed to break apart the connections of these federalist logics. Religious extremism often serves to split the movements in Arab countries; vindictive and racist forms of repression were used to divide the British rioters; and in North America, Spain, and elsewhere in Europe, police provocations to push nonviolent protesters to violence have repeatedly been used to create rifts.

Politics is thus acquiring a plural ontology in these movements. The pluralism of struggles that emerge from differing traditions and express different goals combines with a cooperative and federative logic of assembly to create a model of constituent democracy in which these differences are able to interact and connect with each other to form a shared composition. We have thus seen so far a plurality of movements against global capital, against the dictatorship of finance, against the biopowers that destroy the earth, and for the shared open access to and self-management of the common.

The next step would be to live these new relationships and participate in their construction. Up to this point we have analyzed the *politics* and the *plurality*, but now we would have to explore the *ontological* machine. To do this we have only to enter into the movements' production of subjectivity. Discussing, learning and teaching, studying and communicating, participating in actions—these are some of the forms of activism that constitute the central axis of the production of subjectivity. A plural ontology of politics is set in action through the encounter and composition of militant subjectivities.

Decision. It is very difficult to trace the genealogy of decision making in the multitude and in the movements. Indeed many of the conditions and practices of this process are not visible. Nonetheless, one can grasp the essence of the process by analyzing some of the conditions that were realized by the singular behaviors of the movements of 2011.

Resistance and rebellion are, in fact, some of the initial decisions taken by the movements. Central here are the decisions that anticipate and promote the construction of a common terrain for the activists—the work of agitation, the demonstration, the encampment, and so forth—that is at the base of every collective imagination that supports a movement.

One condition for this process is not only a "being with" but a "doing with" others, which spreads and teaches people how to make decisions. Another decision must be made once the indebted decides not to pay his or her debt; the mediatized decides to break away from media control and media mendacity; the securitized decides to become invisible and learn not to fear; and the represented decides to refuse to be ruled by representatives. It requires a leap from the individual to the collective in order to become an autonomous and participating political subject. This decision must be both singular and common.

It should be obvious that in this context the modern political party—either in its representative, parliamentary form or in its vanguard form—cannot serve as an organ of this kind of decision making. In the past, parties have frequently sought to recuperate the energy and ideals of social movements in order to legitimate their own power. You have done your work in the streets, they tell the multitude; now go home and let us take up the cause in the halls of government. When parties have succeeded in such operations, sometimes benefiting in the next election cycle, they have most often destroyed the movements. Indeed, faced with the movements that erupted in 2011, parties have tried to reclaim and absorb their power, particularly in the countries of the Arab spring, but this is no longer possible. The power of decision created by the movements must reside with those who are acting together politically and cannot be transferred beyond that common terrain. When parties fail to usurp the power of movements, they not infrequently, using their institutional means, repeat the authoritarian and repressive practices that the movements had protested in the first place. But that won't be the end of the story. Even if they disappear from view and from the headlines for a period, the multitudes will inevitably reconvene on a new terrain and find new compositions for expressing their autonomy and power.

Constitutional Examples

Before confronting directly in the next section the discussion of new powers and a new division of power, it will be useful to test the constituent principles and inalienable rights we have elaborated in the context of a few concrete examples. We want to investigate, specifically, how some social goods—water, banks, and education—can be constitutionalized as common and transformed into institutions of the common in line with these principles and rights. The question, in essence, is whether institutions, goods, and resources can be managed effectively in common through democratic participation.

Water. Declaring a resource to be common is not enough. Prohibiting the privatization of water, for instance, and affirming abstractly that it is a common good are not sufficient to make it common and openly available for all to use. This is a lesson we learned from two inspiring social movements: the so-called war on water in Cochabamba, Bolivia, in 2000 and the referendum on water in Italy in 2011. Both struggles prevented the privatization of the public water system, but instead of making it a common resource, as intended, they reinforced public control.

Making a resource like water common requires action on not only the good itself but also the entire infrastructure that supports it. Free access to water requires, in other words, that the complex structures and apparatuses of distribution and filtration are subject to effective democratic management, governed by decisions of the citizens themselves. We refer to citizens here, not users or clients, to emphasize that water and its physical management have to be governed through structures of equal and democratic participation.

In this example, then, the constitutional principle of free access has to be asserted and developed in order for water to become common. In addition, the principle of the sustainability of its use must be taken into account, which means imagining the future as if it were present, and thus valuing the availability of resources for the next generations. And, finally, in order for water to become common, the knowledges of social needs as well as the technical requirements of processing and distribution must not remain the domain of experts (and thus a weapon to be wielded by politicians) but must be spread widely among citizens. Where there is not enough water to satisfy both urban needs and agricultural demands, for example, distribution must be decided democratically by an informed population.

What do I know about water distribution, you might be asking yourself, and do I want to take the time to learn? Knowledge is obviously a prerequisite for democratic participation and management of the common. But one should not exaggerate the complexity of the knowledges required to engage in political decisions regarding our society. People have been trained in apathy and ignorance, encouraged to suppress their appetite for democratic participation and to regard social systems as so complex that only experts can understand them. In previous eras, of course, communities effectively made decisions together regarding the distribution of water and other resources, among the Aymara in the Andes just like in the populations of Holland and the Alps. We need today to stimulate the appetite for these knowledges and rediscover the pleasures of political participation.

It should be clear that making water common does not mean making it public in the sense of assigning its regulation and management to local and state institutions. Common decisions are made through democratic participation not by elected representatives and experts. This distinction raises a core constitutional issue. Public law and public power in the current constitutions are defined in tandem with the private, and they are subordinated to private control with regard to the liberal representative organization of the state. The question of transforming the public into the common thus raises at least three issues initially. The first is an abstract but fundamental principle of making law common, that is, creating a juridical process of the common, which is necessary for the community of citizens to control and administer a good. The second is to create a management system that incorporates the principles of the common uses of goods. And the third defines democratic participation as the political terrain regarding both ownership and management. To speak of common goods, then, means constructing a constitutional process regarding a set of goods managed through the direct participation of citizens.

Making the common the central concept of the organization of society and the constitution is also significant for legal theory. In particular, it helps demystify Rousseau's notion of the "general will," which he conceives as being the will of the people as a whole that stands above and thus transcends the "will of all." A common good that all citizens must manage and make decisions about democratically is not transcendental, like the general will, but immanent to the community. Rousseau the revolutionary, who even denounced private property as a crime, managed to establish the general will as a concept of authority only by imagining that, in order to be of everyone, it has to stand above them all and belong to no one. This is why Rousseau's notion of the general will is susceptible to statist and even authoritarian interpretations. A common good, in contrast, is something that must be constructed, possessed, managed, and distributed by all. Becoming common is a continuous activity guided by the reason, will, and desire of the multitude, which itself must undergo an education of its knowledge and political affects. In order to construct society and generate a constituent process, then, citizens are not obliged to imagine and subordinate themselves to an imperial general will but can create the common themselves through a process that weaves together the will of all.

Banks. In order to realize the constituent principles and inalienable rights of the multitude, banks must become institutions managed in common for the common good, and finance must become a tool for democratic planning. We are not interested here in the question of whether in some future society money could be eliminated, but instead we want to focus on some of the institutional activity required democratically to manage the means of production and regulate the means of exchange. Money serves as a means for the circulation of commodities, for guaranteeing savings and assuring against accidents and misfortune, providing in old age. We will consider below how money must be democratically managed when it becomes a means of investment, but right away we can say that it should be banned as an instrument of accumulation. Money that creates money is the ancient definition of usury, and today such speculative financial practices should be equally reviled.

When we consider the role of banks, several constituent principles come into play that were created by the struggles against indebtedness and insecurity, such as freedom and equality, access to the common, and the sustainability of social relations and development. These principles require that the function of money and the activity of banks are subordinated to the social needs of consumption and reproduction, as well as the promotion of common goods. Banks are always (even in the current neoliberal regimes) institutions of social planning. In liberal and neoliberal regimes, this planning is directed toward guaranteeing and enlarging the means of the private circulation and accumulation of wealth. This is primarily what it means today to call the bank *independent*—independent from the democratic control of citizens. That kind of independence puts the lives and security of others at risk. One of the fundamental measures of the New Deal was to limit risk by separating savings banks from investment banks, but not risking people's savings in speculative operations is not the only problem. More important and more basic today is bringing investments under the control of democratic decision making and the participatory rule of the citizens.

Certainly, after the experience of Soviet socialism, memories of planning and even the notion itself of "the plan" have become infamous, and with good reason. Socialist planning deprived citizens of the freedom to choose and imposed cruel, coercive norms on social reproduction. But one should note that these consequences derived not so much from the techniques of planning but rather from the public and political powers that deployed them. Our antipathy for public powers and our suspicion regarding public law derive in large part from the perverse effects of these failed experiences. The public, an authority that transcends the social, always acts in a bureaucratic way, often irrational, blind, and suffocating. We thus reject the role of banks under socialist regimes as bureaucratic instruments of social planning, but we equally refuse the capitalist model of banks aimed at expanding profit and rent—both of which act against the common.

The rejection of the bank as an instrument of either private accumulation or public planning opens up avenues for conceiving new models oriented toward the accumulation of and planning for the common. In our era of biopolitical production and cognitive capitalism, some of the central productive forces, such as those that work with ideas, affects, code, communication, and the like, are not concentrated in factories but are spread out across the social terrain. Indeed the metropolis is one privileged site where these forces reside and interact. In this context, banks, in coordination with finance capital, appear on the market as central agents to "gather together" collective social competencies and to "integrate" fragmented knowledges in order to make these productive capacities available to business. In effect, finance capital still operates according to the relationship between banks and business as it did in the industrial era, despite the changed conditions of production, and this is one factor that has led to recent economic catastrophes. We need to imagine how these functions of gathering together competencies and integrating knowledges can be put to use in a democratic planning of social production and reproduction. Production must be understood not as isolated to limited, separated domains, such as the factory, but as spread across the entire society. In the interests of the common, then, the bank would not disappear but instead its functions to register, foster, and support the whole range of productive social relationships would have to be increased and enlarged.

This is how the constituent principles of freedom and access to the common can penetrate the banking institution, making it a buttress of other democratic institutions. It is clear that today struggles have to assail the banks and the finance industries to denounce the injustices of their practices, including the ways they increase social insecurity, exacerbate social inequalities, and restrict freedoms. Tomorrow, however, the struggles will have to find ways to transform the banks and the instruments of finance, bending them to fulfill the functions necessary to plan the production, reproduction, and distribution of social wealth through democratic participation.

Education. In order to make education an institution of the common, we need to try to apply the three principles that guided us in the examples of water and banks: make resources common, develop schemes of self-management, and subject all decisions to procedures of democratic participation. Knowledge is a common good par excellence, and education relies on access to knowledge, ideas, and information. Creating schemas of open access to these goods is obviously a prerequisite for any notion of education as an institution of the common.

But education is not only or even primarily about knowledge. When we study we certainly gain knowledge, learn facts, and work with ideas, but above all we foster our intelligence; that is, we develop and train our power to think. In this sense education is at its most basic always self-education. No one can study for you, and the power to think is always already within you. Your intelligence needs to be cultivated. Self-education, of course, doesn't mean getting rid of teachers or tearing down the schools. It means instead that these relationships and institutions have to be oriented toward creating environments conducive to study. The greatest gift a teacher can give is the recognition that each student has the power to think and the desire to use that intelligence to study. Study is the essence of self-education, and unfortunately, it is all too rare in the current forms of education. Self-education must be organized as an instance—perhaps the paradigmatic instance—of open access to the common, including information, knowledges, tools of study, and so forth, free from financial obstacles as well as those of dogmatism and censorship.

Self-education, though, should not be confused with individual isolation. The type of self-education we have in mind bears some similarities to Rousseau's *Émile* but has significant differences. Émile gains a poetic and sentimental education through a training of the senses and interaction with first the physical world and later the realm of ideas and books. The kind of self-education we are discussing is similarly affective as well as social and scientific, but the primary difference is that it is not individual. We can only study in relation to and in interaction with others, whether they are physically present or not. Education in this sense is always an exercise in and demonstration of the equality of singularities in the common. As we study, in other words, we constantly recognize the intelligence of others and learn to benefit from it. It should perhaps be no surprise that Rousseau's Émile, when he meets his future mate, Sophie, immediately imagines her to be his inferior. Self-education as we conceive it, instead, requires a cooperative project of developing our common intelligence.

The management of knowledge must be guided, then, like that of other resources, by the principles of open access, equality, sustainability, and participation. Democratic decision-making structures must replace the present forms of planning that determine the development of education. Today education, especially higher education, is strongly guided, and funding is the primary planning mechanism. As state funding has decreased for public education (most dramatically throughout Europe and North America), private funding becomes a central force in planning. Universities are becoming more corporate, in other words, not only regarding their internal hierarchies, management styles, and reward systems, but also and above all in that corporations that fund research and education effectively determine the management of knowledge and the planning of education.

One of the great US government projects of education planning was inspired by the Soviet launch of the *Sputnik* satellite in 1957. The following year, believing that the Soviet advance in the space race indicated that US education in science and math had fallen behind, Congress passed the National Defense Education Act to dramatically increase funding at all levels of the education system, with applied mathematics, engineering, and sciences as the primary beneficiaries. Even though national security was the explicit rationale for the project, the strengthening of the education system and its guidance toward these areas of study also coincided with the perceived needs of industry at the time—and indeed it is not difficult to trace the ways in which this boost to education benefited US business in subsequent years. The funding also had myriad unintended effects, fostering education in numerous areas.

More than a half century later, how can we imagine today a comparable act of educational planning and an influx of funding? It is worth noting that although corporate funding still focuses on the sciences according to the old industrial model, the needs of business in our present age of biopolitical production are equal or greater in areas of linguistic, communicational, and intellectual development that are typical of humanities education, whose funding has dramatically decreased. But if education were to become an institution of the common, the interests of society as a whole, not those of business, would have to be the guide. Democratic, participatory structures of decision making would have to be established to plan and fund education, develop opportunities of study, and open access to knowledge. That is the kind of educational institution that could be built on the constituent principles.

From the public to the common. When facing the threat of privatization, the struggle for the common often tends to slide toward or even require a defense of public control. Is it necessary, when facing the powers of private property, to struggle for public property when our aim is the common? It seems so, for example, in the battles of students and professors against the privatization of the university and the defunding of secondary education. Their primary and immediate recourse appears to be to reassert the power of the public. Similarly, public power seems to be the primary alternative when confronting the private exploitation of natural resources in many parts of the world, such as diamonds in Sierra Leone, oil in Uganda, lithium in Bolivia, or tar sands in Canada. To combat the private exploitation of the corporations, often foreign owned, that funnel wealth into the hands of the few and, in the process, destroy the social and natural environments, it seems that the most effective weapon is to affirm state sovereignty and make the resources public property. Even more dramatically, when confronting threats of environmental disaster, such as climate change, insisting on state controls and regulation appears as our only option to the continuing destruction wrought by private corporations.

We set out aiming for the common but find ourselves back under the control of the state. It's a misdirected voyage, like Christopher Columbus sailing for India but ending up in the Americas—but that analogy's not really right. It's more like the Soviets who, battling capitalist domination, thought they were headed for a new democracy but ended up in a bureaucratic state machine. What kind of bargain are we making when we struggle for the common but settle for the rule of public property and state control? Once we succeed, are we then stuck with state rule, which brings us no closer to the democratic management of the common?

We see two paths for encouraging and cultivating the passage from public property to the common and from state control to democratic self-management. The first is modeled on the "difference principle" that John Rawls proposes in his theory of justice. According to this principle, inequalities in the distribution of goods should be permitted only if they benefit the least advantaged members of society. In every social decision, other factors being equal, preference should be given to benefit the poor. This principle is intended to set up a dynamic that gradually but consistently tends toward the equal distribution of wealth. A difference principle for the common would work in parallel fashion: every social function regulated by the state that could be equally well managed in common should be transferred to common hands. Proposals for the self-management of aspects of educational life, for instance, such as individual classes or study programs, should be given preference over state management. Similarly, the common, democratic management of natural resources should always take priority when it is at least equally effective and efficient. This kind of difference principle seems to us useful as a theoretical guide but not effective enough to guarantee a real social transformation.

The second path for ensuring a steady movement from the public to the common, which is more active and practical than the first, involves a double combat. Many social movements for the common and against neoliberalism struggle *for* the public to overthrow the rule of private property and, at the same time or sequentially, militate *against* that public power in the interests of the common and mechanisms of self-management. These two paths are not exclusive, of course. They can be combined together and with other strategies. The point is that we do not need to reject all strategies that affirm public control, but neither can we be satisfied with them. We must find the means to set in motion a dynamic that ensures a movement toward the common.

There are many contemporary examples of double struggle, for and against the public. Student movements against the privatization of education often take this character, as do many environmental movements. The paradigmatic example of this double movement in our view involves the dynamic between social movements and progressive governments in Latin America, which is worth analyzing more closely.

Progressive governments and social movements in Latin America. From the 1990s to the first decade of this century, governments in some of the largest countries in Latin America won elections and came to power on the backs of powerful social movements against neoliberalism and for the democratic self-management of the common. These elected, progressive governments have in many cases made great social advances, helping significant numbers of people to rise out of poverty, transforming entrenched racial hierarchies regarding indigenous and Afro-descendant populations, opening avenues for democratic participation, and breaking long-standing external relations of dependency, in both economic and political terms, in relation to global economic powers, the world market, and US imperialism. When these governments are in power, however, and particularly when they repeat the practices of the old regimes, the social movements continue the struggle, now directed against the governments that claim to represent them.

A quasi-institutional relationship has thus developed between social movements and governments. Throughout the twentieth century, socialist practices established a typology of such relationships as *internal* to the political structure—the dynamic between trade union and party, for example, was internal to the functioning of the party, and when in power, socialist governments configured the activities of social movements as within their ruling structures. That internal relation derived from the fact (or assumption) that the union, the party, the social movements, and the government operated according to the same ideology, the same understanding of tactics and strategy, and even the same personnel. The slogan "fighting and in government" promoted by socialist parties conceived these two functions as compatible and internal to the party.

The socialist tradition that posits such an internal relationship between social movements and parties or ruling institutions, however, has been broken. Instead, one of the characteristics we have observed in these Latin American countries during this period is the decisive *externality* and thus separation of the social movements with regard to organizational practices, ideological positions, and political goals. At times the movements and the governments conduct battles together against national oligarchies, international corporations,

or racist elites, but even then they maintain a separation. The
"identity" of the movements is grounded in specific local situations, such as the indigenous communities, the landless peasants who struggle against the latifundios, the unemployed who
demand a guaranteed income, or workers who demand self-
management of production. But at the same time the movements maintain cooperative or antagonistic relationships (or
both simultaneously) with the government so that they can act
autonomously on specific economic, social, administrative, and
constitutional issues.

    This external relationship between movements and govern-
ments has the power to set in motion a significant transformation (and diminution) of the directive aspects of
government action. It could, in other words, force the mechanisms of government to become processes of governance;
the sites on which different political and administrative wills
are engaged can become multiple and open; and the governing function can dilute sovereign power to become instead an
open laboratory of consensual interventions and plural cre-
ations of legislative norms. Most interesting here is the fact
that the multiplicity of encounters, and sometimes conflicts,
maintains nonetheless a deep political coherence of the governmental process. Many aspects of an "institutionality of the
common" emerge here with clarity: the "destituent" force with
respect to the old colonial or bourgeois constitutions; the pre-
eminence of ethical and political programmatic aspects of a
new constitution (being "in another place"); the slow temporality and the autonomy of political developments; the insistence on the transparency of the institutions and
communication; the expression of implicit counterpowers,
which are internal to the constitutional process itself and al-

ready are ready to be wielded, in case of emergency, against the causes of danger; the increased protection of minorities; and the democratic decision-making processes that guide and coordinate all these aspects.

Note that the plural operation of politics we are describing here, with an open relationship between social movements and governments, is not a form of populism. Populist governments manage to combine the diverse expressions of social movements with the sources of sovereign power so as to make an opaque, potentially demagogical mixture. Even when social movements maintain their identities in a populist framework, as is often the case, they must accept being part of a higher synthesis and being subsumed within a hegemonic power. Hegemony is essential to any populist government. When social movements maintain an *external* relationship to the government, however, and defend their autonomy, often through actions against the government, the bases of any such populist hegemony are undermined.

The external relationship between social movements and progressive governments that exists in several Latin American countries—in varying degrees and varying forms—serves for us as a "constitutional example." This is not an exceptional phenomenon whose significance is limited to Latin America. Instead we view this example as a model for other countries and regions. It is difficult to think of a path toward both democratic participation and a new constituent process of the common that does not pass through this experience of an open dynamic of constituent power in action. An open relationship between movements and governments, a plural form of governance with multiple entry points, and an indefinite formation of rules for the forms of life that we invent: these are some of the elements that constitute the procedural horizon of a participatory democracy of the common.

Agenda for New Powers and New Divisions of Powers

The US Constitution has often been celebrated as a perfect instrument of government, "a machine that would go of itself." It's clear today, however, that not only the US Constitution but all republican constitutions are machines that sputter and stop, that get jammed up, that continually break down. From the standpoint of the constitutional principles and truths posed by the movements, it is not difficult to recognize their shortcomings.

The republican constitutions are in desperate need of profound reform, but can they be transformed to create new spaces and structures of democracy? Does the principle of the rule of private property and capitalist markets, which is deeply embedded in the constitutional structures, pose an unavoidable obstacle to any opening to the self-management of the common? These questions and these doubts about the possibility of democratic reform, we find, undermine some of the central positions of the traditional Left, whose most progressive elements remain tied to the defense and reform of the republican constitutions. We thus want, in light of the current crisis, to sketch some aspects of the contemporary constitutional predicament, which we will approach, following convention, by considering in turn the three primary branches of government.

The powers of the executive have expanded considerably in the last decades. The executive bureaucracy has developed structures that effectively double and rival the other two branches. In the United States, for example, decisions of legal experts of the executive branch tend to take precedence over those of the judiciary; the executive's Office of Legal Counsel rivals the importance of the attorney general's office; and the president's economic experts predominate over legislative powers. Similarly in Europe, for some time now, governments have hollowed out parliamentary powers through legislation by decree; interior ministers and police are increasingly free from parliamentary controls; and war powers and the management of the military have been shifted from the legislative to the executive branch.

Why, then, given this disproportion of executive power with respect to the other branches, has not Barack Obama (to take an example, but one could name many others) been more successful completing his reform agenda? Obama did not put an end to the exceptional powers that George W. Bush's administration wielded. Why, then, was he not able to use them effectively? To what extent was Obama himself prisoner of those executive structures? Obama, of course, is no revolutionary, but he did come to office with the intention of effecting some modest, but significant, reforms. The same dilemma can be seen in terms of the Left in Europe. For an example of a major social reform conducted by the Left, one would have to go back to the first two years of the Mitterrand government in France.

The legislative branch, which in many respects should be the source of reform, has been progressively emptied of its constitutional functions. The crisis of democratic representation certainly marks one major weakness of the constitutional arrangement. Legislative powers now have a very weak, almost nonexistent ability to propose social projects, manage budgets, and above all control military affairs. The primary role of legislatures, in fact, has become providing support for or creating obstacles to executive initiatives. It seems that the US Congress's greatest activity, for example, is to block the projects of the executive and to bring to a halt the functioning of the government.

In this context, when the Left entrusts its hopes to the legislative branch (and this is often the only available space), it is inevitably frustrated and disillusioned. People's sense of alienation continues to grow with respect to political parties, which are the backbone of parliamentary representation, and the mistrust of leftist parties is especially strong. The tasks required of parties from the twentieth to the twenty-first centuries, of course, have become extraordinarily complex: in addition to the classical problems of the representation of civil society are problems of government debt, migrations, energy politics, climate change, and so forth. Faced with such complexity their capacities of representation should extend and become more specialized. In reality, though, their representative capacities vanish. The parliamentary system, infested with lobbies, proves to be totally inadequate for these tasks. How can it be reformed or renewed? Is it possible to create new forms of representation and a new terrain of civil debate in which a constituent process could be built from below? The traditional Left has no response to these questions. Debates about reforming electoral systems invariably go nowhere. In Europe, in particular, in discussions about electoral laws it is difficult to distinguish between irony and cynicism. The leftist parties are completely incapable of confronting the dominant role that money plays in electoral politics, both through direct campaign contributions and through the media, which is increasingly becoming the means of expression for the rich and powerful. Their pretense of representing society disappears behind the power of money. And, thus, perhaps paradoxically, corruption becomes, especially for the Left, an almost unavoidable path to election.

The power of the judiciary has, in fact, been mobilized on numerous occasions to determine a new constitutional equilibrium and open reformist avenues. In the United States, for instance, such attempts have occasionally succeeded: the jurisprudence of the Supreme Court in the 1930s and 1960s contributed to social reform movements and helped enact progressive and antiracist reforms of the US Constitution. Those occasions, however, were dependent on exceptional conditions of not only economic crisis but also powerful social conflict that put the social order in danger. Today things have changed substantially, and the power of the judiciary has returned to a conservative position. Without mentioning the crucial role of the Supreme Court in the 2000 presidential election, it is enough to cite the 2010 Supreme Court decision to lift restrictions on corporate spending in elections, considering such contributions to be protected under the right to free speech. In Europe, too, there have in the past been attempts to forge the judiciary into a constituent machine, endeavors to revive an old Jacobin utopia, which are never effective and always ambiguous. In Italy, in particular, the effort to enact reforms based on the power of the judges produces a deformation of the constitutional position attributed to the judiciary, and when these judges do not function along conservative lines, they merely serve as surrogates for political powers. And that creates no end of disasters.

The parties of the Left have thus become parties of lament. They lament the destruction of the welfare state, the imperial military adventures, the incapacity of business to put people to work, the overwhelming power of finance, and the greed of bankers. Eventually they also lament the corruption of their own representatives and their own lack of representative legitimacy. The only position they know how to take aggressively is the defense of the constitution, protecting an imaginary past consecrated, for example, by sanitized versions of antifascism in Europe or civil rights in the United States, both of which are corralled into a constitutional compromise with ruling financial powers. They suffer from an "extremism of the center," which often rests for them on reminiscences of an idyllic past.

The problem is not only that the traditional Left is incapable today of launching an effective dynamic of constitutional reform. The republican constitutions themselves can no longer be reformed or redeemed. A new constituent process is needed to transform the constitutional order and social terrain. We see the foundation from which to initiate such a process in the principles and truths constructed by the movements. Although we are in no position to sketch even the broad outlines of this unknown terrain, based on what we have analyzed thus far we can distinguish some of its characteristics. As a first approach, then, let us preserve for explanatory purposes the three traditional constitutional functions—legislative, executive, and judiciary—and investigate how they might be transformed by the new constituent principles.

Legislative. A legislative power in a constituent process must be not an organ of representation but one that facilitates and fosters the participation of all in the governing of social life and political decision making. It fact, in many historical instances as far back at least as the eighteenth century, legislative assemblies have successfully launched such constituent experiments. In these moments, which have often been brief, politics was brought down to the level of social reality and reconfigured according to the expression of social needs and desires. In several contemporary cases, too, such as some of the Latin American experiences we cited earlier, constituent assemblies have played an innovative role by bringing together and giving expression to a range of social forces. The legislative face of a constituent power must reflect *and* embody the multiplicity of social movements and social forces and thereby interpret the plural ontology of politics.

Federalism is thus a fundamental principle of a constituent legislative power. By *federal* here we do not mean a central authority ruling over smaller political units such as states or provinces. Instead we understand *federal* in a more basic sense as an open, extensive relation among diverse political forces spread across the social terrain and not subsumed under an abstract, centralized unity. The shape of federalist organization as we intend it, in other words, is not pyramidal but horizontal and extensive. Such a federalism fosters the plural and process-oriented dimensions of politics.

Is it possible to make these "post-state" aspects of federalism the basis for a legislative power that is not closed and centralized? This begins to take form when we think of a legislative power as following the temporality of the social movements and adjusting its federal structures to their spatial dimensions, which are at once local and widely disseminated. The complexity of this arrangement, in fact, becomes productive: the networks can serve to measure and weave together in relation to the singular dimensions of legislative functions.

The assemblies established in the encampments and occupied squares of 2011 spread power in such a federalist fashion. Each assembly functions according to its own rules and develops its own techniques for expression and decision making. In some cases simple mechanisms are used, such as shaking your hands in the air or following on Twitter to show approval for a proposition. The assemblies all share, though, the intention to disrupt the ingrained tendencies to centralize power in a small group of leaders, and instead they provide a mechanism by which all can be included in deliberation and decision making. The assembly form, in other words, serves as a tool for creating a democratic legislative power in these movements among hundreds and sometimes thousands of participants. The assemblies, of course, have not always fulfilled the aspirations for equal and democratic participation during their brief existence, but they do nonetheless present a powerful model for thinking about a possible federalism.

Taking the assemblies as a model for a federalist legislative power immediately raises a question of scale. How can their form be extended beyond the confines of the square to society as a whole? The skeptic responds that, just as we learn from ancient Greece, democratic decision making is possible only among a small and limited population. Throughout modernity, though, numerous projects have sought to extend participation in decision making widely across society, which, even when not ultimately successful, suggests strategies that we might pursue today.

Several twentieth-century socialist initiatives, for example, sought to spread power in a federalist manner by putting power in the hands of workers and constructing the means for workers to make political decisions themselves. Workers' councils constituted the central proposition of all streams of socialism that, contrary to the authoritarian currents, consider the primary objective of revolution to be democracy, that is, the rule of all by all. At least since the Paris Commune, the workers' council in its many variants, such as the German *rat* or the Russian *soviet*, has been imagined as the basis for a federalist legislative power. Such councils and the forms of delegation they institute serve not so much to represent workers but instead to allow workers directly to participate in political decision making. In many historical instances, of course, these councils functioned in a constituent way only for a brief period. In some cases, as in the Weimar Constitution, they were neutralized and made into organs of industrial comanagement, and in others they were imagined falsely to be the basis of a workers' dictatorship that would after a transitional period somehow give way to democratic governance. Despite such failures, though, the vital element of workers' councils is their attempt to incarnate a legislative power in the field of production, destroying the separate realm of politics and politicians, and instead spreading the circuits of political decision making widely through the networks of workers. The great power of workers' councils resides in the fact that they activated and utilized already existing relationships among workers in the factories: the same circuits of communication that functioned in production were repurposed in the political structures of the councils.

We certainly wouldn't propose resurrecting workers' councils in their twentieth-century form. One of their obvious limitations is precisely that they were restricted to a portion of society: even the participation of all industrial workers would leave out of the political process waged workers in other sectors, the families of workers, the unemployed, and others.

That said, however, some fundamental characteristics of contemporary production allow us to reimagine the basic function of workers' councils in a broader and more democratic form. When the production of codes, languages, ideas, images, and affects is, as we claim, increasingly central in contemporary biopolitical production, the boundaries that delimit the realm of production are expanded and blurred such that all of society tends to be brought within its networks. In this context, then, if we extend the structures of decision making and political participation along the lines of production, as the old workers' councils did, we could potentially achieve a much broader reach and bring into political structures a much larger portion of society. The structures of relation and communication created in biopolitical production, in other words, could be repurposed to extend the assembly form to a broad social level.

Creating effective political structures that trace biopolitical production in this way is, of course, not an easy task, and it raises a series of additional questions. It is, however, a way to begin to interpret the lessons of "the squares" and their experiments with assemblies in order to apply them on a social level. The key task of generating a new legislative power remains that of inventing a federalist form to extend political participation in decision making across the entire social terrain.

Finally, any effort to democratize society and include all in decision making has to struggle against the deeply ingrained distaste for politics among large portions of the population that has long been promoted by those in power. Before any democracy is possible, there must be a new production of political affects that cultivates people's appetite for participation and desire for self-government. The encampments of 2011 were one important step in that direction. They were populated not only or even primarily by experienced activists but instead by people new to such forms of political action, and through their experiences, their desires to create and participate continually grew. The surest and most powerful way to generate democratic political affects is by practicing democracy.

Executive. An executive power in a constituent process must address the needs for social and economic planning and development. Modern and contemporary forms of planning and development, however, have been widely and justly criticized. In order to imagine and enact a new executive power, we have to recognize first how traditional concepts and practices of planning and development change when the common becomes their focus and when decision making is conducted through democratic, participatory procedures.

The forms of planning practiced by state socialism died a miserable death, and as we said earlier, no one should mourn or seek to resurrect them. The cruelty and ineffectiveness of these practices were primarily a result of the centralization of the decision-making power. Socialist bureaucracies served both to maintain the separation and isolation of those in the center (blocking the centripetal flow of social forces) and to administer the directives throughout society (facilitating the centrifugal flow of command).

Recognizing the brutality of state socialist planning, though, should not blind us to the injustices of and disasters created by capitalist planning, which are often hidden and mystified. The neoliberal and neoconservative revolutions of the last decades of the twentieth century propagated the myth of a weak state, claiming to reduce state powers and pull the state out of the social field—getting government off our backs. State expenditures for social welfare were indeed reduced, but, in fact, total state budgets only grew due to increased funding to military, legal, and business interests. The neoliberal state, despite claims to the contrary, wields strong planning powers, which it enacts through close collaboration with corporate and financial interests. No one should be fooled anymore by the democratic aura that neoliberals still hope to evoke when they claim that the market decides. The decision-making market in such statements is a euphemism, at best, for the forces of wealth, including the banks and financial powers, that wield formidable instruments of planning. They determine, for example, what software will be developed, what dams will be built, who will buy a house, and so forth. During normal periods finance and banks operate relatively autonomously from the state, but in the end their profound connection always surfaces. In fall 2008, at the height of the financial crisis, the theater of the collaboration of US government officials and the captains of Wall Street provided a peek behind the curtain and showed how small the circle of decision makers actually is. In any case, the current crisis is another demonstration of the disasters created by capitalist planning. And thus we can easily sympathize with those who, recognizing the socialist and capitalist catastrophes, might want to have nothing to do with planning in any form.

The concept and practices of development are in equal disrepute. Throughout the twentieth century, development was conceived primarily as growth according to an industrial model, with the assumption that human well-being is dependent on continually producing more goods and consuming more resources. It is now abundantly clear that such growth has created a system that couples extraordinary waste in dominant parts of the world with deprivation in subordinated parts and, further, that the planet cannot survive this trajectory. Development conceived as growth in this industrial mode—more automobiles, more commodities, more fields for agriculture, and so forth—is clearly not sustainable. Despite the fact that enormous populations in many parts of the world still lack for goods and food, some people, focused on the unsustainable nature of the current trajectory, thus advocate reversing the processes of growth and abandoning notions of development.

The bleak scenario we have laid out regarding planning and development shifts substantially, however, when we recognize the centrality of the common, that is, the earth and its ecosystem—the forests, the seas, soil, air, water, and so forth—as well as the products of social labor, including ideas, images, codes, information, affects, and much more. As we argued earlier regarding water, however, resources are not immediately or spontaneously common. A project of organization and infrastructure is required for us to have open access to a shared resource. For water to become common requires pipes, pumps, and management systems, whereas for ideas to become common requires education, publication forums, and so forth. Just as the common must be organized in order to free up access, it must be managed in order to be sustained for the future. The well-being of the earth's atmosphere, as well as the realm of ideas and indeed all forms of the common, requires planning.

What does development mean when the common becomes central to economic and social life? It certainly doesn't always mean growth. It means instead constructing mechanisms so all can share in, have access to, and participate equally in the production of our common wealth. Administration takes on a completely different form in this context. Throughout capitalist (and socialist) modernity, when industrial production served as the regulative model, economic administration required bureaucratic organization together with hierarchical structures of control and discipline in order to organize productive cooperation. The administrative needs are very different for biopolitical production, which activates our intellectual and affective capacities to produce ideas, codes, social relationships, and the like. Productive cooperation in the biopolitical realm tends to be created in social networks among producers without the need for bureaucratic oversight and guidance. This does not mean that no administration is necessary but rather that it has to be immanent, woven into the social fabric itself.

We have presented this new, constituent executive power separate from the legislative power for clarity of explanation, but really the two must be completely intertwined. The executive functions of planning, in other words, must be configured in a federalist way such that all can participate democratically in decisions. This raises immediately an objection regarding expertise, which we posed earlier. Just as political affects and the appetite for participation will have to be fostered in order to realize the demands of a constituent legislative power, so too will knowledge and expertise about our social world have to be cultivated on the broadest scale. The politicians and financial moguls who today make decisions are not geniuses delivered to us from heaven. There is no reason that through education we cannot all become at least as expert as they are regarding our natural, social, and economic worlds in order to make informed, intelligent decisions.

Judicial. With respect to the legislative and the executive we have been able to reinterpret their functions as a means to explore the nature and organizational needs of a constituent process. Considering how judiciary power can be configured in such a project, however, requires that we clarify and disentangle some of its primary elements.

We should recognize, first of all, that judiciaries, despite claims of independence, are always political powers. The spectacle of nomination hearings of US Supreme Court judges is one demonstration of that fact. And their political character is often abundantly clear when judges attempt projects of social reform or when they attempt to block the initiatives of one of the other branches. It is not uncommon to hear politicians attack the judges as political when they disagree with their views and laud their wisdom and independence when they agree. Even in the rare instances when the judiciaries act in a progressive direction, for example, to force the racial integration of schools or protect voting rights of minorities or workers' rights to organize, their interventions take an authoritarian form and effectively usurp the power of parliamentary and representative bodies, resulting ultimately in all kinds of disasters.

Our inclination is not to seek ways to make the judiciary truly independent but rather to admit that certain functions of the judiciary are inevitably political and discover how these can be adequately reconfigured on the political terrain. We are not thinking here of the tasks of administering civil and criminal law. In these domains judges and juries must be as independent as possible from partisan pressures, and here indeed one would have to embark on the challenging task of eliminating the political character of law. We want to focus instead on some of the constitutional functions of the judiciary.

One central constitutional function of the judiciary is to provide checks and balances on the government. The ability to check, though, requires difference. When the members of the judiciary are not substantially different from those of the other two branches, that branch can provide only weak mechanisms to check the others. The primary difference currently provided by the judiciary, in fact, is temporal, since they are not subject to periodic election, and this generally has the effect of creating stability through not so much balance but inertia. It seems to us that if a constituent legislative power were created according to federal and participatory principles that extend decision making throughout society, then it would provide a much more substantial field of differences. In other words, in an open and constituent assembly structure, diverse and conflicting forces serve to check one another, creating a dynamic balance. One might worry that in such a configuration the position of the judiciary as a "third" power, external to the others, has been lost and swallowed into the one legislative-executive governance structure. The differences among those who participate in the constituent process, however, and the externality of each to the others is far greater and thus more effective than a separate governmental body.

Another primary constitutional function of the judiciary is to interpret the constitution. In the context of the kind of constituent power we are imagining here, such interpretation is still essential. The inalienable rights we proposed earlier as fundamental principles—including liberty, happiness, free access to the common, the equal distribution of wealth, and sustainability—require interpretation to be applied and enacted. The question is whether we need a small group of experts in black robes to interpret them for us. If a constituent power is to take a democratic and participatory form, then constitutional interpretation, too, will have to be socialized. The principles and truths on which the constitutional process is based, after all, were not handed down from on high but were constructed through the movements and dynamics of society itself. Here again, as we said earlier, a widespread educational project is necessary to develop the intelligence, create the political affects, and furnish the necessary tools of expertise to enable the entire multitude to participate in such interpretation and decision making. But we see no reason why this should be beyond our capacities.

We have no presumption to write a new constitution, and we know well that the indications we present here regarding legislative, executive, and judicial power contribute only some general principles and very little content. We have merely attempted to note a few elements that could form part of a future agenda. What is clear from the declarations of the movements that began in 2011, however, is that a discussion about constituting a new society is already mature and has become the order of the day.

Next: Event of the Commoner

We can see the city on a hill, but it seems so far off. We can imagine constituting a just, equal, and sustainable society in which all have access to and share the common, but the conditions to make it real don't yet exist. You can't create a democratic society in a world where the few hold all the wealth and the weapons. You can't repair the health of the planet when those who continue to destroy it still make the decisions. The rich won't just give away their money and property, and tyrants won't just lay down their arms and let fall the reins of power. Eventually we will have to take them—but let's go slowly. It's not so simple.

It's true that social movements of resistance and revolt, including the cycle of struggles that began in 2011, have created new opportunities and tested new experiences. But those experiments, beautiful and virtuous as they are, don't themselves have the force necessary to topple the ruling powers. Even great successes often quickly turn out to be tragically limited. Banish the tyrant and what do you get? A military junta? A theocratic ruling party? Close down Wall Street and what do you get? A new bailout for the banks? The forces piled against us appear so enormous. The monster has so many heads!

Even when tempted by despair, we should remember that throughout history unexpected and unforeseeable events arrive that completely reshuffle the decks of political powers and possibility. You don't have to be a millenarian to believe that such political events will come again. It's not just a matter of numbers. One day there are millions in the street and nothing changes, and another day the action of a small group can completely overturn the ruling order. Sometimes the event comes in a moment of economic and political crisis when people are suffering. Other times, though, the event arrives in times of prosperity when hopes and aspirations are rising. It's possible, even in the near future, that the entire financial structure will come crashing down. Or that debtors will gain the conviction and courage not to pay their debts. Or that people will en masse refuse to obey those in power. What will we do then? What society will we construct?

We can't know when the event will come. But that doesn't mean we should just wait around until it arrives. Instead our political task is paradoxical: we must prepare for the event even though its date of arrival remains unknown.

This isn't really as mysterious as it sounds. Take a lesson from some of the architects and ideologues of the current neoliberal order. Milton Friedman and the economists of the Chicago school had studied neoliberal economic policies, trained students in them, and projected the policies and institutions of a neoliberal order long before the social and political conditions existed to put them into practice—and, indeed, long before the September 1973 military coup led by Augusto Pinochet in Chile. Naomi Klein recounts that when, a few months before the coup, the plotters appealed to Chicago-trained economists, the "Chicago boys," for an economic pro-

gram, they were able quickly to put together a five hundred–
page manual that detailed the necessary steps to implement a
neoliberal economic and social order along the lines of Friedman's thought. Chicago economists did not plan the Pinochet
coup nor did they foresee it, but they were ready when it hap-
pened. Indeed for the implementation of neoliberal policies in
numerous other countries since that time, Klein maintains,
which were all made possible by some form of disaster, there
was ready at hand in each case an economic playbook.

What is instructive about this example is how useful and
effective it can be to prepare for an unforeseen opportunity.
But the circumstances the neoliberals found in Chile are
nothing like the ones we face now. The nature of the opportunity, first of all, is completely different: no coup d'état or
other military action will precipitate an event for a democratic
transformation today. The subject that prepares, second, cannot be a vanguard or a cabal like the Chicago boys but must
instead be a multitude.

This paradoxical task of preparing for an unforeseen event
may be the best way of understanding the work and accomplishments of the cycle of struggles of 2011. The movements
are preparing ground for an event they cannot foresee or predict. The principles they promote, including equality, freedom,
sustainability, and open access to the common, can form the
scaffolding on which, in the event of a radical social break, a
new society can be built. Moreover, the political practices that
the movements experiment with—assemblies, methods of collective decision making, mechanisms for not only the protection but also the expression and participation of minorities,
among others—serve as a guide for future political action.
Much more important, though, than any of the constitutional

principles or political practices, the movements are creating new subjectivities that desire and are capable of democratic relations. The movements are writing a manual for how to create and live in a new society.

We argued earlier that forces of rebellion and revolt allow us to throw off the impoverished subjectivities produced and continually reproduced by capitalist society in the contemporary crisis. A movement of organized refusal allows us to recognize who we have become and to set out on becoming different. It helps us free ourselves of the morality of debt and the work discipline it imposes on us, bringing to light the injustice of the social inequalities of debt society. It allows us to turn our attention away from the video screens and break the spell the media hold over us. It supports us to get out from under the yoke of the security regime and become invisible to the regime's all-seeing eye. It also demystifies the structures of representation that cripple our powers of political action.

Rebellion and revolt, however, set in motion not only a refusal but also a creative process. By overturning and inverting the impoverished subjectivities of contemporary capitalist society, they discover some of the real bases of our power for social and political action. A deeper debt is created as a social bond in which there is no creditor. New truths are produced through the interaction of singularities being together. A real security is forged by those no longer bound by fear. And those who refuse to be represented discover the power of democratic political participation. Those four subjective attributes, each characterized by a new power that revolts and rebellions have achieved, together define *the commoner*.

In medieval England, commoners formed one of the three estates of the social order: those who fight (the nobility), those who pray (the clergy), and those who work (the commoners). Modern English-language usage in Britain and elsewhere has preserved the meaning of the term *commoner* to designate a person without rank or social standing, an everyman or everywoman. The term *commoner* as we intend it here must preserve the productive character that stretches back to medieval England, while taking it further: commoners are not just common for the fact that they work but, rather and more important, because they work on the common. We need to understand the term *commoner*, in other words, as we do the designations of other occupations, such as baker, weaver, and miller. Just as a baker bakes, a weaver weaves, and a miller mills, so, too, a commoner "commons," that is, makes the common.

The commoner is thus an ordinary person who accomplishes an extraordinary task: opening private property to the access and enjoyment of all; transforming public property controlled by state authority into the common; and in each case discovering mechanisms to manage, develop, and sustain common wealth through democratic participation. The task of the commoner, then, is not only to provide access to the fields and rivers so that the poor can feed themselves, but also to create a means for the free exchange of ideas, images, codes, music, and information. We have already seen some of the prerequisites for accomplishing these tasks: the ability to create social bonds with each other, the power of singularities to communicate through differences, the real security of the fearless, and the capacity for democratic political action. The commoner is a constituent participant, the subjectivity that is foundational and necessary for constituting a democratic society based on open sharing of the common.

The action of "commoning" must be oriented not only toward the access to and self-management of shared wealth but also the construction of forms of political organization. The commoner must discover the means to create alliances among a wide variety of social groups in struggle, including students, workers, the unemployed, the poor, those combating gender and racial subordination, and others. Sometimes, when invoking such lists, people have in mind coalition building as a practice of political articulation, but the term *coalition* seems to us to point in a different direction. A coalition implies that various groups maintain their distinct identities and even their separate organizational structures while forming a tactical or strategic alliance. The alliance of the common is entirely different. Commoning does not involve, of course, imagining that identities can be negated such that all will discover they are, at base, the same. No, the common has nothing to do with sameness. Instead, in struggle, different social groups interact as singularities and are enlightened, inspired, and transformed by their exchange with each other. They speak to each other on the lower frequencies, which people outside of the struggle often cannot hear or understand.

This is one lesson we should all be able to learn from the cycle of struggles that began in 2011. The protesters at the Wisconsin statehouse did not delude themselves into thinking they were the same as those in Tahrir Square or that they shared the same social conditions, just as those who erected tents on Tel Aviv's Rothschild Boulevard did not see their reflection in the encampments of Puerta del Sol. While firmly rooted in their specific local conditions, they borrowed practices from each other and transformed them in the process; they adopted each other's slogans, giving them new meanings; and most important, they recognized themselves as part of a common project. The political task of the commoner is achieved through these kinds of exchanges among and transformations of singularities in struggle.

Some of the more traditional political thinkers and organizers on the left are displeased with or at least wary of the 2011 cycle of struggles. "The streets are full but the churches are empty," they lament. The churches are empty in the sense that, although there is a lot of fight in these movements, there is little ideology or centralized political leadership. Until there is a party and an ideology to direct the street conflicts, the reasoning goes, and thus until the churches are filled, there will be no revolution.

But it's exactly the opposite! We need to empty the churches of the Left even more, and bar their doors, and burn them down! These movements are powerful not despite their lack of leaders but because of it. They are organized horizontally as multitudes, and their insistence on democracy at all levels is more than a virtue but a key to their power. Furthermore, their slogans and arguments have spread so widely not despite but because the positions they express cannot be summarized or disciplined in a fixed ideological line. There are no party cadres telling people what to think, but instead there exist discussions that are open to a wide variety of views that sometimes may even contradict each other but nonetheless, often slowly, develop a coherent perspective.

Don't think that the lack of leaders and of a party ideological line means anarchy, if by anarchy you mean chaos, bedlam, and pandemonium. What a tragic lack of political imagination to think that leaders and centralized structures are the only way to organize effective political projects! The multitudes that have animated the 2011 cycle of struggles and innumerable other political movements in recent years are not, of course, disorganized. In fact, the question of organization is a prime topic of debate and experimentation: how to run an assembly, how to resolve political disagreements, how to make a political decision democratically. For all those who still hold passionately to the principles of freedom, equality, and the common, constituting a democratic society is the order of the day.

Notes

We thank those friends who helped us with the preparation and publication of this pamphlet, including Lisl Hampton, Melanie Jackson, Sandro Mezzadra, Jedediah Purdy, Judith Revel, Gigi Roggero, Raúl Sánchez Cedillo, Nico Sguiglia, and Kathi Weeks.

Opening: Take Up the Baton

"Who knows but that, on the lower frequencies, I speak for you?": See Ralph Ellison, *Invisible Man* (New York: Vintage, 1947), 581.

Chapter 1: Subjective Figures of the Crisis

The Indebted

We find four recent books particularly useful for analyses of the political significance of debt in contemporary society: François Chesnais, *Les dettes illégitimes* (Paris: Raison d'agir, 2011); Richard Dienst, *The Bonds of Debt* (New York: Verso, 2011); David Graeber, *Debt: The First 5,000 Years* (New York: Melville House, 2011); and Maurizio Lazzarato, *La fabrique de l'homme endetté* (Paris: Editions Amsterdam, 2011).

"Freedom, equality, property, and Bentham": See Karl Marx, *Capital*, vol. 1, trans. Ben Fowkes (New York: Vintage, 1977), 280.

The Mediatized

"The problem is no longer": See Gilles Deleuze, "Mediators," in *Negotiations*, trans. Martin Joughin (New York: Columbia University Press, 1995), 121–34, 129.

See Étienne de La Boétie, *Discourse on Voluntary Servitude* (New York: Columbia University Press, 1942); and Baruch Spinoza, *Theological-Political Treatise,* in *Complete Works*, ed. Michael L. Morgan, trans. Samuel Shirley (Indianapolis: Hackett, 2002).

"*Living information* is continually produced": See Matteo Pasquinelli, "Capitalismo mecchinico e plusvalore di rete," *UniNomade 2.0*, 17 November 2011, http://uninomade.org/capitalismo-macchinico/; unless otherwise noted, all translations are our own. See also Romano Alquati, "Composizione organica del capitale e forza-lavoro alla Olivetti," part 1, *Quaderni rossi*, no. 2 (1962); and part 2, *Quaderni rossi*, no. 3 (1963).

Karl Marx, *The Eighteenth Brumaire of Louis Bonaparte* (New York: International, 1963), 123–24.

The Securitized

"The prison begins well before its doors": See Michel Foucault, "Le prison partout," in *Dits et écrits*, vol. 2 (Paris: Gallimard, 1994), 193–94, 194.

For current statistics on US prison populations, see the Sentencing Project, www.sentencingproject.org.

Michelle Alexander, *The New Jim Crow: Mass Incarceration in the Age of Colorblindness* (New York: New Press, 2010).

On the relation between growing prison populations and neoliberal economic strategies, see Loïc Wacquant, *Punishing the Poor* (Durham, NC: Duke University Press, 2009).

"We have the wolf by the ear": See Thomas Jefferson, letter to John Holmes, 22 April 1820.

The Represented

"To represent means to make present an absence": See Carl Schmitt, *Verfassungslehre* (Berlin: Duncker und Humblot, 1928), 209.

Chapter 2: Rebellion against the Crisis

Hannah Arendt, *The Human Condition* (Chicago: University of Chicago Press, 1958).

"Une force séparée de ce qu'elle peut": See Gilles Deleuze, *Nietzsche et la philosophie* (Paris: Presses universitaires de France, 1962), 140.

Invert the Debt

"The individual carries his social power": See Karl Marx, *Grundrisse*, trans. Martin Nicolaus (New York: Vintage, 1973), 157.

Break Free

Angela Y. Davis, *Are Prisons Obsolete?* (New York: Seven Stories Press, 2003).

"A free man thinks of death least of all": See Baruch Spinoza, *Ethics*, part 4, proposition 67.

Constitute Yourself

For an exemplary project to redeem the US Constitution, see Jack Balkin, *Con-*

stitutional Redemption: Political Faith in an Unjust World (Cambridge, MA: Harvard University Press, 2011).

Regarding the concept of destituent power (*poder distituyente*), see Colectivo Situaciones, *19 and 20: Notes for a New Social Protagonism*, trans. Nate Holdren and Sebastián Touza (New York: Minor Compositions, 2011).

Chapter 3: Constituting the Common

Declaration of Principles
We are attracted by those streams in US constitutional theory that interpret the principles contained in the Declaration of Independence as the real and legitimate basis for the Constitution. One potent source of this line of thinking is Abraham Lincoln's enigmatic 1861 "Fragment on the Constitution and Union," in *The Collected Works of Abraham Lincoln*, vol. 4, ed. Roy Basler (New Brunswick: Rutgers University Press, 1953), 168–69.

Constituent Struggles
Peter Linebaugh, *The Magna Carta Manifesto: Liberties and Commons for All* (Berkeley: University of California Press, 2009).

Constitutional Examples
On study and self-education, see Marc Bousquet, Stefano Harney, and Fred Moten, "On Study," *Polygraph*, no. 21 (2009): 159–75.

On the difference principle, see John Rawls, *A Theory of Justice* (Cambridge, MA: Harvard University Press, 1971), 75–83.

Agenda for New Powers and New Divisions of Powers
"A machine that would go of itself": See Michael Kammen, *A Machine That Would Go of Itself: The Constitution in American Culture* (New York: Knopf, 1986). Kammen borrows the title from an 1888 essay by James Russell Lowell.

On the expansion of the executive branch, see Bruce Ackerman, *The Decline and Fall of the American Republic* (Cambridge, MA: Harvard University Press, 2010).

On the predominant role of corporations and the creation of an "inverted totalitarianism," see Sheldon S. Wolin, *Democracy Incorporated: Managed Democracy and the Specter of Inverted Totalitarianism* (Princeton, NJ: Princeton University Press, 2008).

Next: Event of the Commoner
Naomi Klein, *The Shock Doctrine: The Rise of Disaster Capitalism* (New York: Metropolitan Books, 2007).

For analyses that use the term *commoner* in ways allied with our own, see the journal the *Commoner* (www.commoner.org.uk) as well as the work of authors identified with it, such as Massimo De Angelis, George Caffentzis, and Silvia Federici.